THE FINAL STRAW

THE FINAL STRAW

A Study in the Gospel of Mark

E. L. GORDON

ⒸiUniverse®

THE FINAL STRAW
A Study in the Gospel of Mark

iUniverse books may be ordered through booksellers or by contacting:

iUniverse LLC
1663 Liberty Drive
Bloomington, IN 47403
www.iuniverse.com
1-800-Authors (1-800-288-4677)

ISBN: 978-1-4917-2065-3 (sc)
ISBN: 978-1-4917-2066-0 (e)

Library of Congress Control Number: 2014901177

Printed in the United States of America.

iUniverse rev. date: 07/22/2014

Contents

Acknowledgements

Whatever we accomplish in life there is a wind beneath our wings. I want to thank my grandmother, Dorothy Fry, my wonderful family, Dolores (wife) Ebonee and Jamin (daughters), Keshawn, Khmyah, Marlee, Kobe, and Zayre (grandkids), Presiding Elder Lemon and Mrs. Lemon, Presiding Elder Sneed and Mrs. Sneed, the Tuggersons, Marie Dixon-Jones, Rev. James T. Golden, Dr. James E.A. Stephens, Margaret and Theodore Hunter, Walter and Mary Simmons, the members of St. James AME Church, Savannah, Ga, St. Paul AME and Greater Turner Tabernacle AME, Macon Ga, and other churches I have served, Seminary professors Drs. Kenneth Henry, Mark Ellingsen, Wayne Merritt, Temba Mafico, and Carolyn Knight, and my dad. I also want to thank Faith, Perseverance, Prayer, Adversity, Doubt, Frustration and You Can't Do It. All of these have been the wind beneath my wings. But if it had not been for the Lord on my side . . .

To God be the Glory: Ernest L. Gordon aka Pastor "G"

A Word from the Author

The Gospel of Mark is the most exciting of the gospel writings. It is the story about Jesus of Nazareth, the Servant of Man, and Son of God with power. Mark portrays Jesus as a radical revolutionist constantly in conflict with Israel's religious leaders. Mark is pictorial, vivid, and imaginative. Mark's gospel starts out like an action packed movie. Mark allows the reader to follow Jesus' Galilean ministry as he moves the story along with words like "straightway" and "immediately". No sooner than Jesus comes up out of the water from being baptized the Devil shows up with a proposition.

Shortly thereafter, Jesus chooses a motley crew of fishermen, tax collectors and militant radicals to become his disciples. Jesus calls them with the promise to make them fishers of men. The disciples follow Jesus up and down the dusty roads of Israel. They hear firsthand the words that fall from his lips. They are eyewitnesses to Jesus' miracles. They are there when Jesus heals the sick, casts out demons; calms raging seas, feeds the multitudes, and raises the dead. Their commitment to follow Jesus earns them each the title, Apostle.

However, Jesus' teachings and miracles causes tension with the religious leaders of Israel and Jesus flees to Bethany out of the watchful eye of Pharisees and Sadducees. The disciples' lives winds-up in peril. They go from becoming "fishers of men to bearers of the cross." The disciples did not expect Jesus life to end the way that it did.

"The Final Straw" is a study of the Gospel of Mark that reveals how the ongoing controversies between Jesus and the religious leaders and the events in Jerusalem at Passover spiraled into a conspiracy of murder. "The Final Straw" is an exciting read for anyone interested in the life of Jesus through the eyes of Mark.

After serving as a pastor for many years, preparing Bible studies, as well as, as a professor at Savannah State University and Mercer University I decided to put the pen to work and use these skills to write a study on the Gospel of Mark. I am certain that people from all walks of life will find the study highly useful for understanding, teaching and preaching the Gospel of Mark.

Read the highlighted Bible passage and the lesson. The lesson review is for discussion. Several charts on the parables and miracles of Jesus recorded in the Gospel of Mark have been provided for further study. Read the highlighted Bible passage and the lesson. The lesson review is for discussion. Several charts on the parables and miracles of Jesus recorded in the Gospel of Mark have been provided for further study. Well! I know you are going to enjoy reading "The Final Straw." Go ahead and get started. Be blessed and grow in grace!

Introduction to the Gospel of Mark

Matthew, Mark, Luke and John are called the Gospels. Matthew, Mark and Luke are known as the synoptic gospels, from the Greek word synopsis, meaning seeing together.[1] They tell similar stories about Jesus. Some of the same stories told by Mark can also be found in Matthew and Luke. John conveys certain events different from those recorded in Matthew, Mark and Luke. The Gospels tell about the works, deeds, teachings, and miracles of Jesus Christ of Nazareth. They convey the story about Jesus' life, death, and resurrection.

The second gospel was written by John Mark. Mark was born in Cyrene, Africa. Mark was not a disciple of Jesus, but he was privy to the many works and deeds done by Jesus. It is likely that Mark had seen and heard Jesus at some time during his ministry. Mark was also involved in the infancy of the early church by entertaining prayer meetings in his home, (Acts 12:12). Biblical scholars believe that Mark was the cousin of Barnabas, whom we read about with Paul in the Book of Acts. Mark also traveled with Paul and Barnabas until a disagreement arose between he and Paul (Acts.12:12; 25; 15:36-40; Col. 4:10; II Tim. 4:9-11). Even though tension arose between Mark and Paul, it was Mark that Paul sent for when others abandoned him, (Acts 12:25, 15:36-40, 2 Tim.4:9-11).

Mark also traveled with Peter in Rome and served as his secretary, (I Pet.5:13). Mark founded a Church in Alexandria and became the church's first bishop. The date of Mark's death is uncertain. Tradition says Mark died a martyr and was dragged through the streets of Alexandria.[2]

The Gospel of Mark: The word "gospel," means "good news." **The gospel is the message preached by Jesus and the disciples about the good news of the kingdom of God that leads to salvation, and eternal life.**[3] Mark is writing about the good news of Jesus Christ. When Jesus appears on the scene he announces the good news of the kingdom of God. The Gospel of Mark was written between 55 and 70 AD. Although Matthew is the first book in the New Testament, it was not the first gospel written. The Gospel of Mark was written before Matthew, Luke, and John. The Gospel of Mark is the earliest of the gospel writings. Biblical scholars also believe that Matthew and Luke may have used Mark's gospel to write their own accounts about Jesus of Nazareth. The gospel writers did not write on site. The disciples were not taking notes as Jesus preached and taught in the synagogues. The Gospel of Mark was written years after Jesus' ascension. Mark's gospel is believed to have been written during Nero's reign as emperor of Rome, 54-68 AD. Nero was a cruel, strewed leader that persecuted Christians. He was regarded as one of Rome's worst emperors, (Mark 8:34).[4]

The Style of Mark's Gospel: Mark's gospel starts off running! Up pops John the Baptist preaching in the wilderness of Judea and Mark is off to tell the story of Jesus of Nazareth, the Galilean preacher, and servant of God. The Gospel of Mark centers upon Jesus' Galilean ministry. Jesus often traveled back and forth between Galilee and Judea. The Gospel of Mark is the shortest of the gospel writings with sixteen chapters.

However, Mark differs from the other two synoptic writers in that Mark does not have a birth story about Jesus. Jesus is thirty years old when we meet him at the Jordan River and is baptized. Mark tells the story of Jesus of Nazareth in a very simple, but detailed way. For example, both Matthew and Luke record many of the parables spoken by Jesus. John records short sayings spoken by Jesus. Mark, however, moves us with Jesus.

Mark's gospel is a story of action, energy and excitement. Mark tells what Jesus did. Mark uses the words "straightway" and "immediately" more than forty times. In The Gospel of Mark, Jesus is servant leader. Mark 10:45 is the theme passage. "For the Son of Man came not to be ministered unto, but to minister and to give his a life a ransom for many."[5] Mark introduces Jesus as the Suffering Servant, the Son of Man, and the Son of God with power. Mark is writing to a community of people who knows what it means to suffer and to serve. He is writing to slaves and slave owners. He is writing to a subject people. The Roman Empire was the world power of Jesus' day. Gentile Christians in the early church were experiencing persecution in the Roman Empire. Mark writes to encourage them to be faithful to Christ in the midst of suffering. He tells them the story of Jesus' trial, suffering, death, burial, and triumphant resurrection. Mark suggests that even Rome is subject to the higher power of the Kingdom of God. Since Mark is writing to Gentile Christians who are not always familiar with Jewish customs, Mark adds his own commentary to shed light on certain Jewish customs, words, and phrases (Mk. 3:17; 5:41; 7:2-4).

Parables in the Gospel of Mark: Parable means to set beside. A parable is a simple story used to illustrate a spiritual or moral lesson. Flanders defines parable as an arresting short story taken from everyday settings to illustrate or make memorable a single teaching.[6] There are nine parables recorded in the Gospel of Mark. Jesus taught in parables for several reasons. Jesus used parables to teach kingdom living, (Mk.4:33-34). He used parables to point out the nature of the kingdom of God. Jesus also used parables to point out the hypocrisy of Israel's religious leaders (Mk.4:1-20).

The Parables of Jesus Recorded in Mark

The Parable of the New Cloth on an Old Garment	Mk.2:21
The Parable of New Wine in Old Wineskins	Mk.2:22
The Parable of the Sower	Mk. 4:1-9
The Parable the Lamp Stand Under a Bushel	Mk. 4:21-22
The Parable of the Growing Seed	Mk. 4:26-29
The Parable of the Mustard Seed	Mk. 4:30-32
The Parable of The Wicked Husbandman	Mk. 12:1-12
The Parable of the Fig Tree	Mk. 13:28-32
The Parable of the Landlord	Mk. 13:33-37

Mark's Messianic Secret:

Mark identifies Jesus as having power over sickness, disease and demons. Throughout Mark's gospel we witness Jesus' power at work as he calmed the raging sea, the raging soul of a man possessed by demons, a woman with a raging issue of blood and a father's raging distress over his dying daughter. Jesus even demonstrated power to raise the dead. Mark uses Jesus' power to raise the dead to alert us to what is to come. However, Mark's gospel has an air of suspense. Jesus often told those that he healed to keep it a secret. The secrecy of Jesus' identity in the Gospel of Mark is referred to as the "Messianic Secret." In 1901, William Wrede noticed that in Mark's gospel account Jesus sought to keep his identity a secret and proposed the messianic secret motif. The Messianic Secret refers to an often made statement by Jesus in the Gospel of Mark in which Jesus commanded his disciples and many of those he healed to remain silent about his messianic mission. Mark keeps his audience in suspense until the crucifixion where the truth about Jesus comes out when the sun refuses to shine, the moon turns as blood, the earth quakes, the Temple curtain is rented, and a Roman soldier cries out, "Surely this is the Son of God." The Messianic Secret is unveiled! [7]

Mark's Messianic Secret

Jesus heals a man with leprosy	Mk. 1:43
Jesus heals a man's withered hand	Mk. 3:11-12
Jesus raises Jarius' daughter	Mk. 5:43
Peter's confession	Mk. 8:30

Miracle Stories in Mark

The miracles recorded by Mark reveal Jesus' authority in the spiritual and physical realm. The feeding of the multitudes reveals Jesus' power to provide (Mk.6:30-44). The healing stories reveal Jesus' power to heal physically. The demon stories reveal Jesus' power to heal spiritually. The storm stories reveal Jesus' power over nature and the distance plus the danger that Jesus will endure to deliver us from the storms of life (Mk.4:35-41; 6:45-52).

Miracle Stories Recorded in Mark

The Gadarene Demoniac	Mk.5:1-20
Jesus Raises Jairus' Daughter	Mk. 5:21-24; 35-43
A Woman with an Issue of Blood	Mk.5:24-34
Jesus Feeds the Five Thousand	Mk.6:30-44
Jesus Walking on Water	Mk. 6:45-56
Jesus Heals a Deaf Man	Mk. 7:31

5

Jesus Feeds the Four Thousand	Mk. 8:1-13
Jesus Heals a Demon Possessed Boy	Mk. 9:14-29
Jesus Heals Blind Bartimaeus	Mk.10:46-52

Cultural Setting of the Gospel of Mark

In the first century AD, the time in which Jesus lived, the Roman Empire ruled the world. Tiberius Caesar was emperor of Rome, Pontius Pilate was governor of Israel, and Herod Antipas was tetrarch of Israel. Both Jews and Gentiles lived in Israel. For example, a certain area of Galilee was referred to as Galilee of the Gentiles. Regarding religious leaders of Israel, Caiaphas was the high priest and Pharisees and Sadducees were the major players in the religious, social, and political arena. Most likely those that lived in the time of Jesus of Nazareth were exposed to at least four languages: Hebrew, Greek, Aramaic and Latin. Most Jewish boys learned Hebrew in the classroom of the synagogue. However, Aramaic, a language related to Hebrew was commonly used after the Jews returned from Babylonian Exile. Each region in Israel had its own dialect of Aramaic. A person from Judea could recognize the distinct dialect of a Galilean (Mk. 15: 66-70, Matt. 26: 69-75, Lk. 22: 54-62). Latin was the language of the Romans, whereas Greek was the primary language of the empire and was most likely heard and spoken in various settings. Jesus and the disciples, as well as the populous of Israel were exposed to a multiplicity of languages and cultures. The fact that Greek was widely spoken throughout the Roman Empire made it possible for the spreading of the Gospel.[8]

Outline of Mark

John the Baptist, Jesus Baptism, and Temptation, 1:1-13
Jesus in Galilee-1:14-6:6a

Jesus in Galilee and other cities-6:6b-9:50
Jesus Goes to Jerusalem-11:1-13:37
Jesus Passion and Resurrection-14:1-16:8

The Gospel of Mark is a non-stop venture of excitement that spirals into a conspiracy of controversy, hatred and murder. Every footstep Jesus takes leads to Calvary. The religious leaders of Israel refuse to stop until Jesus of Nazareth is dead. The disciples panic and run! The Devil and the forces of evil celebrate for a season. However, Jesus' resurrection changed the game! The disciple's faith is renewed when the resurrected Christ shows up and commissions them to go into the world and preach the good news of the kingdom of God.

Lesson Review

1. When was the Gospel of Mark written?

2. To whom is the author writing?

3. What does the word "gospel" mean?

4. Who is Mark writing about?

5. Which gospel was written first?

6. What is a parable?

7. What is the Messianic Secret?

Holy Rollers

Jesus and his parents, Joseph and Mary, were among the masses of people and caravans that made the yearly visit to Jerusalem at Passover. People from all over the Roman Empire visited the Holy City during Passover. Passover was a time of celebration. When the Israelites were slaves in Egypt, God told Moses to have everybody kill a lamb and spread the blood on the door post because He was sending the Death angel to slay all of the first born males in Egypt. Moses said that when the Death angel saw the blood he would pass over. The episode of that final night in Egypt was preserved in the Passover and celebrated each year and told generation after generation. Since then, the Jews always celebrate Passover.

Every young Jewish boy wanted to go to Passover and see the great fire rise from the gigantic brazen altar in the Temple at Jerusalem as the high priest made sacrifice for the sins of the people. Males age twelve and older were required to attend Passover. No doubt Jesus got an eye full each time he went to Jerusalem for Passover.

It was almost three o'clock in the evening. In just a few minutes three trumpet blasts would signal the official beginning of the Passover.[9] Joseph Caiaphas, the high priest, put on his priestly garments. He wore a magnificent blue robe, accented with blue, purple, and scarlet pomegranates and golden bells, which jingled as he moved. Around his waist was a blue, purple and scarlet band interwoven with spun gold. Caiaphas took the breast plate adorned with twelve colorful stones that represented the twelve tribes of

Israel and hung it across his chest. He then carefully took the head dress, a fine linen turban wreathed with blue, and a golden crown and placed it upon his head. On the crown was written, "Holy to the Lord." At the third blast of the trumpet the procession began to move. Joseph, Mary, and Jesus could see the long, long procession ahead as the high priest led the people to the upper court in the Temple of Jerusalem. **The Temple of Jerusalem was the place where Jews offered religious sacrifices and offerings.**[10]

The Temple was marvelous to look upon. It was erected by King Herod the Great in 20B.C. as an act of kindness toward his hostile Jewish subjects. The Temple was the crowning jewel of Jerusalem. The white marble stones covered with plated gold, glistened in the sunlight. The Temple was built with a number of courts. The Court of Priests was where the priests and Levites entered to offer sacrifices. [11] The huge doors were covered with Babylonian tapestry of blue, purple, crimson, and gold to depict the heavens. Above was a golden vine, the symbol of the nation of Israel. There were two rooms in the sanctuary. The first was the holy place which contained a golden altar for incense, a golden table for the bread offering and a golden menorah lit by seven lamps burning pure olive oil. The second room, the Holy of Holies was separated by a heavy linen curtain embroidered in gold. Only the high priest was allowed to enter the sacred place on the annual Day of Atonement. [12]

The Court of the Gentiles was where both Jews and Gentiles could go and come. It was about 35 acres large. However, this was as far as Gentiles were allowed to go. A warning sign was posted in Greek and Latin that stated, "No Foreigners Allowed."

The court was always busy and crowded with people. Merchants selling doves, lambs, and cattle for sacrifices set up in the Court for the Gentiles. Money changers set up shop there and transacted the business of converting foreign money into Jewish shekels. Jesus listened at Pharisees, scribes, and rabbis discuss points of the Mosaic Law in the Court of Gentiles (Lk. 2:46). Pharisees and

Sadducees were the two major religious groups in Israel. They ran things and called all the shots.

Pharisees were the religious leaders of Israel that emphasized strict interpretation and observance of the Mosaic Law.[13] Pharisees tried to live separately from the world. Pharisee" means separatist. They stressed purity and strict adherence to the Mosaic Law. Their piety set them apart from other people. Pharisees were protectors and interpreters of the Law of Moses. Moses was a national hero in Israel because he led the Israelites out of Egypt. He received the Law directly from the hands of God on Mt. Sinai. Wherever the Law was silent Pharisees filled in the gaps and gave interpretation through oral tradition. Pharisees believed in the spirit world. They believed in angels. They also believed in a resurrection and life after death. Pharisees also had oversight of the synagogue.[14] After the Jews returned from exile in Babylon they set up synagogues throughout Israel wherever at least ten men gathered to read the scriptures. The synagogue became the primary place for teaching and reading the Hebrew Scriptures.[15] The masses looked up to Pharisees as the perfect example of piety and righteousness. However, Pharisees had a disdain for people that had not reached their level of spirituality. Even though Pharisees controlled the synagogues and defended the Law, their teachings were hypocritical and burdensome. These images were etched into the mind of Jesus.

The Sadducees also left an indelible impression upon the young Jesus. **The Sadducees were the religious leaders of Israel associated with the priestly, aristocratic class. They accepted the written Mosaic Law and rejected oral traditions. They had over sight of the Temple.**[16] A small group of Sadducees believed to have connections with King Herod were called Herodians (Mk.3:6). Sadducees were the liberal and wealthy ruling class. Sadducees did not believe in the spirit world. Neither did they accept the oral traditions of the Law. They only recognized the written Law of Moses. Sadducees wielded a great deal of political power because they had favor with Rome for not rocking the boat.

However, Pharisees criticized them for their tolerance of Roman rule. Sadducee and Pharisees were often at odds with each other over religious matters.[17]

Sadducees controlled the Temple in Jerusalem and the Sanhedrin Council. The Sanhedrin Council was seated in Jerusalem. The council was made up of seventy religious leaders both Pharisees and Sadducees. They were divided into three groups: chief priests, elders and scribes. The Sanhedrin Council met to decide important cases and rule on disputed points of religious law. They met in a place called the Hall of the Hewn Stone. Caiaphas, the high priest, was also the head of the Sanhedrin Council.

The Romans realized the tremendous power of the Sanhedrin Council and the high priest and set laws in place to curb their authority. One safeguard was that the marvelous blue robe worn by the high priest was kept in the custody of the Romans. Before 63B.C. the king of Israel was also the high priest. The Romans recognized the authority that the robe symbolized and therefore seized it and housed it in the Fortress of Antonia.[18] A stairway and an underground passage way connected the fortress with the Court of the Gentiles. Six hundred Roman soldiers were stationed in the Fortress of Antonia and were always on the alert for disturbances in the Temple precincts. A Roman garrison would be stationed in the same place when Jesus visits the Temple years later.

The Romans abolished the kingship and made the office of high priest an appointed position subject to the approval of Rome. Rome also withheld the Sanhedrin Council's authority to decide executions and to carry out the death sentence. However, the high priest remained the most powerful figure in the nation of Israel.[19] Therefore, Sadducees took no chances at losing favor with Rome. The religious leaders of Israel were "holy rollers!" They walked around in their long robes looking pious and righteous. They refused to let anything and anyone under-mind their power and authority.

Jesus got a glimpse of the religious leaders at work. He witnessed the overwhelming presence of Roman rule in Israel. He saw the tension between the Pharisees and Sadducees. He saw their hypocrisy. On the journey back home there was always talk about what had gone on at Passover, how the Pharisees and Sadducees pretended to be holy and did business in the Temple. No doubt these images became etched in the mind of Jesus as he made the annual pilgrimage to Jerusalem at Passover.[20]

Lesson Review

1.   What religious holiday did Jesus and his parents attend?

2.   Where was the Temple located?

3.   Who had the Temple built?

4.   Discuss a major religious or political holiday you celebrate

5.   List and discuss the two primary religious groups of Jesus day.

The Beginning of Jesus Ministry

The beginning of the gospel of Jesus Christ, the Son of God. As it is written in the Prophets: "Behold, I send my messenger before your face, who will prepare your way before you."

"The voice of one crying in the wilderness:

'Prepare the way of the Lord; Make His paths straight.'"

John came baptizing in the wilderness and preaching a baptism of repentance for the remission of sins. Then all the land of Judea, and those from Jerusalem, went out to him and were all baptized by him in the Jordan River, confessing their sins. Now John was clothed with camel's hair and with a leather belt around his waist, and he ate locusts and wild honey. And he preached, saying, "There comes one after me who is mightier than I, whose sandal strap I am not worthy to stoop down and loose. I indeed baptized you with water, but He will baptize you with the Holy Spirit."

(Mk.1:1-8, NKJV).

John the Baptizer

The Gospel of Mark opens with a passage spoken by the Old Testament prophet, Isaiah (Isaiah 40:3). Isaiah was one of the great prophets of Israel. He prophesied to the Kingdom of Judah for a span of forty years. He witnessed the rise and reign of four kings: Uzziah, Jothan, Ahaz, and Hezekiah. However, Isaiah announced that before the Messiah came a bold prophet was coming to prepare the way. Isaiah described the coming of this bold and powerful prophet as a voice crying in the wilderness.

According to Mark, John the Baptist was the fulfillment Isaiah's prophecy.[21] There is a peculiar story behind the birth of John the Baptist told by Luke (Lk.1-5-25). John the Baptist was the son of Zacharias and Elizabeth. Zacharias and Elizabeth were descendants of Aaron, Moses brother. The sons of Aaron and all male descendants served as Levitical priests. Zacharias served as a priest in the Temple. Zacharias and Elizabeth wanted a child. However, Elizabeth was barren. Zacharias and Elizabeth prayed for the Lord to bless them with a child. Years passed and still no answer from the Lord. The clock was ticking! Time was winding-up. Time after time they came up empty. Zacharias and Elizabeth were swiftly moving beyond the age for having children. The possibility of a child looked dismal. In biblical times, Hebrew women were often scorned and mocked when they were unable to have children. Barren women were believed to be outside of God's favor. Jewish Rabbis said that seven people were out of favor with God. The list began, "A Jew who has no wife or a Jew who has a wife and has no child.[22] Imagine the girl talk in the hair and nail salon. "Girl, I sure feel bad for Mrs. Elizabeth. All these years and she still has not had a baby. Something is wrong somewhere." Imagine the guys engaged in small talk over a cold . . . while watching a football game. "Hey, man what's going on with Zacharias? He can't seem to get that first kid?" In those days, people had many children. Jacob had twelve sons. In these times of busy schedules and blooming careers, one to three children are more than enough (Gen. 11:30, Gen. 29:31, I Sam. 1:1-11, Lk.1:7).

However, Zacharias and Elizabeth lived in different times. Therefore, Zacharias and Elizabeth prayed that the Lord would show them favor. They prayed and prayed, but nothing happened. Zacharias and Elizabeth wondered why the Lord had not answered their prayers. They did the right things. They loved the Lord. They served the Lord with all their heart and soul. They kept the Lord's commandments, yet the Lord had not answered their prayer.

What happened to the "Preferred Believers Card" that we should get when we come on the Lord's side? It looks like when we give our time and energy to live for the Lord and promote the Lord's work our name should be at the top of the list. It looks like we would get preferred treatment from the Lord. It looks like the Lord would Fed-Ex the answer when believers pray. However, there are times in life that we still come up empty in spite of the good we try to do and our long hours of prayer. There are times when we pray and the Lord does not answer right away. There are even times when we pray and the Lord does not respond the way we want. Contrary to popular belief, the Lord always answers prayer. The Lord may say, "yes, no, or wait awhile." Even though Zacharias and Elizabeth did not get an immediate response to their prayers, they continued to exercise faith and hope. They did not give up. They kept trying. They kept praying. They kept trusting and serving the Lord. It is easy to walk away from the Lord when we are not getting our way. Too often people give up and quit when the answer is right around the corner. It would be good if we could see around the corner when our patience is wearing thin.

One day, something strange happened while Zacharias was serving in the Temple. Gabriel showed up with a message from the Lord. Gabriel is the Lord's messenger angel. Gabriel is the Lord's courier. Whenever the Lord needs to get a message out Gabriel is the one that delivers it. Gabriel is always in God's presence. Gabriel is in the room when the Heavenly Council is in session discussing plans for the believer. Gabriel is privy to heavenly and holy conversation. Gabriel told Zacharias, "I was in the room when the Lord was talking and your name came up, (Luke 1:19)." That is awesome! Imagine that if you will when you pray. There is no telling how many people are praying at any given time. However, of the millions of people in the world waiting for an answer to their prayers your name came up.

Unlike Job, whose name also came up in the Heavenly Council for the sake of being tested and tried and becoming the victim of trouble and calamity. Zacharias name is called that the Lord might bless he and his wife Elizabeth. Gabriel said to Zacharias, "The Lord heard your prayer and Elizabeth is going to have a child." This is shouting news. This is a hallelujah, thank you Jesus, glory to God moment. This is a moment for Zacharias to get his praise on. Instead of Zacharias running and jumping into Gabriel's arms and giving him a big kiss on the cheeks, a big hug, or "high five," Zacharias did not believe what Gabriel told him. He told Gabriel that Elizabeth was too old to have children. When Gabriel had heard enough of Zacharias' doubting, he silenced him. Gabriel said, "You will call him, John (Lk.1:13)." Sometimes we can talk too much and delay the blessing that God has for us. Perhaps if you can't say anything positive just keep silent. The Lord silenced Zacharias until John was born. John the Baptist was a miracle baby. John's parents were up in age and beyond child bearing when he was born. The Lord is still producing miracle babies—babies that were not supposed to make it, babies that others either gave away or threw away, babies that grew up to be successful and productive even though society had written them off. The birth of John the Baptist is the evidence of what fervent prayer can do.

It is interesting that after we pray and bother the Lord over and over again for something and the Lord finally responds in our favor we find it hard to be true. We should pray in faith and expect an answer. My grandmother, Mama Fry, often told me the story of how sickly I was as a baby. She said I was born with asthma and that I cried all night so that she could not sleep. She said, "Since I couldn't sleep I just prayed all night. Before I knew it you would fall off to sleep." To this day, I have the slightest clue what an asthma attack is like. Grand Ma's prayers changed things! No matter how long it may take for the answer to come, keep praying.

John grew up to be one of the most popular and powerful preachers in Israel. They called him "the Baptizer" because he preached a message of baptism and repentance. John the Baptist did not have a church with fine church furniture, poly-glass pulpit, big screens, plush carpet, state of the art sound system and all the fixings of today's churches. John the Baptist was a simple preacher with a simple message. Repent! John was not the glorified TV preacher lavished with gold and a ring on every finger. He was not a fashionable preacher dressed in tailored made three button and four button suits with cuffs at the bottom. You would not see John the Baptist wearing a Brooks Brothers, Shaffner Marx, Steve Harvey, Magic Johnson, Sean John, Russel Simons PhatPharm, or FUBU suit line. He did not have a selection of Stacy Adams, Bostonians, Mezlan, David Eden, or exotic skinned shoes. John the Baptist wore camel hair and sandals. He ate locust and wild honey. John the Baptist preached in the wilderness of Judea. The wilderness is not only definitive of a geographical location, but also a spiritual condition. When John the Baptist started preaching the people were spiritually weak. They were spiritually destitute. However, John turned the wilderness into a place of worship and an oasis of hope. The word of the Lord came to John the Baptist in the wilderness. Do not underestimate where you are. You may be in a place isolated and secluded from other people. You may be in the boiler, the storage room, the warehouse, or a room somewhere at the end of the hall and nobody knows your name, but God has a GPS system that can find you wherever you are.

John was a bold preacher. He did not bite his tongue. He did not talk out of both sides of his mouth. He did not back down from the truth. John the Baptist preached a message of repentance and forgiveness of sins. John preached the same message to everybody, rich and poor, men and women, scribe and sinner, Pharisee and Sadducee, rabbi and robber, harlot and house wife, bond and free. "Repent!" **Repent means to have a change of mind and a change of heart in regards to sin. Repent means to show sorrow for sin, to turn from sin and return to God.**[23] Too often people hear the gospel preached and leave the same way they came. They leave with the same bitterness, the same hostility, and the same attitude. Repent means that we have a change of attitude. John the Baptist told the people to repent and get right with God. He urged the people to prepare the way for the coming of Christ and the kingdom of God. Many people came out to hear John the Baptist. They came from Judea and Jerusalem. They repented of their sins and were baptized in the Jordan River. The Jordan River was not far from where John the Baptist preached. Those that were baptized showed that they wanted to be forgiven of their sin. Baptism signified a change of heart with the intent to live better lives for the Lord. That is what baptism and repentance should mean today; to turn and have a change of heart that encourages us to live better lives for the Lord.

Take me to the Water: Jesus is Baptized

However, someone bigger and bolder than John the Baptist was coming. John the Baptist was the forerunner. He was no match to the preacher that was coming. He was not even worthy to untie the man's shoes. One day, Jesus got word that John was preaching and baptizing in the wilderness of Judea. The time had come for Jesus to close his carpentry shop, put away his tools and answer his calling. Jesus was thirty years old when he was baptized and began his ministry. Jesus went down to the Jordan River and after talking with John for a moment he was baptized. Jesus said this made everything right. Jesus does not tell us to do anything that he has not already done. He does not send us anywhere he has not gone. "Follow me" is Jesus' watchword.

The crowd watched as Jesus was baptized. God was also watching! This was a proud day for Jesus' Father to see his son baptized. God showed how pleased he was by putting on a special effects show. Heaven opened. Light shined from heaven. A dove passed over Jesus and released the anointing of the Holy Spirit, and the voice of God spoke from heaven "This is my beloved son in whom I am well pleased". What a statement! What might God say about you or me? This is my beloved servant in whom I am well pleased; always serving, always encouraging, always lifting, and always giving. Or might we be an embarrassment to the Lord?

The religious leaders were also watching when Jesus was baptized. They were there keeping an eye on John the Baptist. They were at odds with John the Baptist because of his bold preaching. John called them vipers and hypocrites. John's preaching got him into trouble. No doubt, the Pharisees and Sadducees breathed a sigh of relief when they got the news that King Herod had John the Baptist beheaded. However, even though John the Baptist was put to death, word soon reached the masses about Jesus of Nazareth.

An Appointment with Satan

Satan was also watching. He invited himself to Jesus' baptism. He heard God brag on Jesus. He saw heaven open and the anointing fall. He saw the special effects show that God put on for his son. There is nothing that angers Satan more than hearing God brag on the believer. Bragging is what caused Job to have a hard time. "Have you considered my servant Job, that there is none like him in all the earth (Job 1:8)?"

As soon as Jesus' baptism ceremony was over, Satan was there to see what Jesus was really made from. He took Jesus into the wilderness and tested him for forty days. Satan wanted to break Jesus before his ministry got started. He tried to kill Jesus at birth, when King Herod had all the first born males of Israel killed (Matt.2:16-21).

Satan will use everything and everybody at his disposal to undermind the work of kingdom building. Jesus' temptation in the wilderness was one of Satan's many designs to hinder Jesus' destiny.

Satan is a master of timing. He tempted Jesus at his weakest moment. Jesus was hungry and tired after fasting for forty days. Satan tried to get Jesus to compromise. He told Jesus there was a short cut to where he was trying to go. The short cut to hunger was turning stones into bread. The short cut to getting down from the mountain was jump and angels will catch you. The short cut to power was, "bow down to me!" Satan is a Bible scholar. He is masterful at manipulating the Word of God and planting seeds of doubt. There are at least three explicit examples in the Bible of Satan's ability to distort and twist the word of the Lord and create doubt in the mind of the believer.

First, in the Garden of Eden, Satan twisted what the Lord said and caused Eve to doubt God's command: "Did not the Lord say you may eat of every tree in the Garden? You will not surely die. The day you eat of it your eyes will be opened (Gen. 3:1-4)." Watch this! In the case of Job, Satan had the audacity to try and plant doubt in the mind of God. Satan pushed God to test Job. He suggested that Job served the Lord because the Lord blessed Job. Satan ran down the list of stuff that God had given Job: money, livestock, land, houses, health, children, a wife and friends." Satan propositioned God. "Take some of his stuff and you will see that I'm right. Job will curse you to your face (Job 1:9-12)." Job had no earthly idea that God and Satan were engaged in a discussion and were about to place a wager against him. We seem to forget that Satan is a "son of God and has access to Heaven. He has his own gate key and can come and go as he likes. There are times when God and Satan sit down and have a cup of hot coffee, a cold glass of ice tea, a piece of red velvet cake and ice cream or something and chat about what is going on in the world. God was caught between a rock and hard place because he bragged on Job. "There is no one like him in all the earth." If God is that confident about Job, God has no recourse but to turn Job over that Satan may prove his point.

In the case of Jesus in the wilderness, Satan showed up and tried to under-mind Jesus' identity: Satan is a master at identity theft. He spends all of his time creating ways to turn believers away from their God ordained destiny. Listen to what he says to Jesus. "If you are the son of God . . . (Matt. 4:1-3, Mk. 1:12-13). Three times Satan tried to create doubt in the mind of Jesus. Three times he tried to get Jesus to compromise and make a deal. Satan is always looking for deal makers.

However, Jesus refused to make any deals. Jesus used the word of God to overcome temptation. Each time Satan made a foolish suggestion Jesus responded with "It is written." Every believer is destined to have an appointment with Satan. Sooner or later he will show up peddling his bag of goods. Satan shows up at our weakest moment. He shows up when we are distraught, distressed, lonely, lacking, overwhelmed, and troubled. He will drag us to the window of life and make us look out over the landscape. Look at you! Look at what you are going through! "If you are a child of God why are you going through this?" We cannot do battle with Satan using unproven weapons. The word of God is the most effective weapon against Satan, sin and temptation. The word of God gives us victory over the tactics of Satan. Jesus' victory over Satan in the wilderness confirmed the start of his ministry.

Lesson Review

1. What did Zacharias and Elizabeth pray for?

2. How often do you pray?

3. Have you ever prayed and the answer did not come right away?

4   How do you handle unanswered prayer?

5.   How has your life changed after being baptized?

6.   Discuss a time when you were tempted by something.

A Call to Adventure:

And as He walked by the Sea of Galilee, He saw Simon and Andrew his brother casting a net into the sea; for they were fishermen. Then Jesus said to them, "Follow Me, and I will make you become fishers of men." They immediately left their nets and followed Him. When He had gone a little farther from there, He saw James the son of Zebedee, and John his brother, who also were in the boat mending their nets. And immediately He called them, and they left their father Zebedee in the boat with the hired servants, and went after Him (Mk. 1:16-20, NKJV).

Setting up Camp: Jesus Goes to Capernaum

The Lord never passes us to the next level in life until we pass the tests for the level we are on. Jesus' victory over Satan's temptation in the wilderness prepared him for the next level of ministry. After returning from being tempted by Satan in the wilderness, Jesus began to put his team together and set his ministry into motion. He recruited some men to mold and shape as disciples. Every leader needs a team of committed followers that will assist in advancing the work.

Mark's focus is upon Jesus' Galilean ministry. In Jesus' day, Galilee and Judea were the two primary regions in Israel. Samaria sat in the middle. Much of the action in the Gospel of Mark took place in Galilee. Galilee was a major seaport city located near the Sea of Galilee. Jesus left his hometown Nazareth and moved to the city of Capernaum to set up his ministry headquarters. **Capernaum was also a seaport city, located on the northwest shore of the Sea of Galilee, about 16-20 miles from Galilee.**[24] This was a prime spot for Jesus to launch his ministry since Capernaum served as a major hub for travelers, *Via Maris,* "the way of the sea." Soldiers, merchants, businessmen, peddlers, panhandlers, maidens, and wayfarers, etc. flowed in and out the city of Capernaum.

Choosing a Team: Jesus Chooses the Disciples

After setting up headquarters Jesus called twelve men to be his disciples: Simon Peter, Andrew his brother, James the son of Zebedee and John his brother, Philip and Bartholomew, Thomas, Matthew the tax collector, James the son of Alphaeus and Lebbaeus, whose surname was Thaddaeus, Simon the Canaanite, and Judas, Iscariot, who also betrayed him, (Matt. 10:1-4, Lk.6:12-14). In Jesus' day there were all kinds of disciples and religious and revolutionary movements. **A disciple is a follower of someone else's teaching.** There were the disciples of John the Baptist. The Zealots were a fanatical Jewish movement that fought against Roman rule in Israel. The Essenes was an ascetic community that lived away from mainstream Jews. Christians are disciples for Christ because we follow the teachings of Christ. [25]

Jesus chose the twelve disciples to be with him. He trained them, prepared them and equipped them to go forth to preach and teach the gospel. Jesus' disciples came from different backgrounds and vocations. As Jesus was going along the seashore of Galilee he called four fishermen, Simon Peter, Andrew, James and John. Capernaum may have been the home of Peter, Andrew, James and John. On the other hand, they may have been from Bethsaida, a well know fishing village in Galilee. Bethsaida means "fishing house." However, most of the disciples were from Galilee.

According to Mark, Simon Peter, Andrew, James and John were the first ones Jesus called to be his disciples. The men that Jesus chose to follow him and become his disciples were not from the status quo. They were not white collar workers. They possessed no formal training. They were not from the ecclesiastical or the aristocratic circle. They were outcasts and the least likely to have been candidates for anything that had to do with religion in the eyes of the religious leaders. Some of them were fishermen. Fishermen were not highly looked upon. They were smelly and sweaty. Matthew was a tax collector. Tax collectors worked for the Roman Empire and were disliked and despised by the local town people. Judas Iscariot, James the Lesser and others were Zealots waiting for a chance to overthrow Roman government.

Unfortunately, most of the pictures we see of the disciples portray them as old men. However, contrary to popular belief the disciples were most likely young men. No offense, but imagine twelve old men trying to keep up with the young, energetic, thirty year old Jesus. Jesus was all over the place. One day he was in Galilee. The next day he was in Judea. One day he was preaching in one city and preaching somewhere else the next day. They could not have kept up. Can't you hear them? "Slow down Jesus! Let me catch my breath. I can't get around as fast as I use too. I don't get out at night. You should have come along just a little sooner. You're a day late and a dollar short. But, I'm praying for you."

The men that Jesus chose to become his disciples were a group of misfits. Imagine how they must have looked at each other when Jesus introduced them. "Peter, James, John, meet Matthew." He will be going with us. "Matthew!" "This guy cheated us. We were carrying fish to one of the local markets and this guy said we were overweight and charged us double." Fishermen working with a tax collector! Militant radicals hanging out with fishermen! A tax collector following a preacher! The Lord recruits the most unlikely and the least likely to serve. Not only that, but he places us in difficult positions and encourages us to work with people we do not care much about. If you resent working with people you do not like and care little for, perhaps you have missed one of the Lord's greatest lessons in life.

The disciples were common men called to an uncommon task. They were in for the adventure of a life time. Jesus took his motley crew and began to teach them. "Follow me, and I will make you fishers of men," (Mk.1:16-17). The phrase "follow me" occurs at least thirteen times in the Gospel of Mark. Jesus did not have a formal classroom to train the disciples. He did not have a chalk board, an overhead projector or power point for orientation. They did not have a recommended textbook. He did not give the disciples manuals covering the five steps to laying hands on the sick or the four steps to casting out demons, or what they should say to calm a raging storm.

When I was in the Marines we were given a little red book, called the "Little Red Monster." The Little Red Monster had everything we needed to know as Marines. It had formations, fire team rushes, orders for guard duty, the ten general orders, and a bunch of other stuff. Jesus' disciples were not as fortunate. The disciples were green. They knew nothing about preaching. They knew nothing about casting out demons. It was all on the job training. They learned as they followed Jesus. Sometimes the disciples got on Jesus' nerves because of their lack of faith. Nevertheless, they committed themselves to following Jesus back and forth to Galilee and Judea (Jn.1:43; 2:1-2; 3:22; 4:3-4). They were in for the long haul. They were destined to be eyewitnesses to some strange and miraculous things. According to Mark, after Jesus chose the first group of disciples, he hit the ground running, healing the sick, casting out demons and taking authority over evil spirits, (Mk. 1:21-45).

Jesus Demonstrates Compassion

Jesus was teaching in the synagogue when the disciples witnessed their first demonstration of Jesus' power and learned one of their first lessons about becoming fishers of men. (Mk. 1:21-45). **The Synagogue is the place where Jews gather on the Sabbath for worship and religious instruction in the Jewish faith. Jesus taught in the synagogue and the Temple.**[26]

While Jesus is teaching in the synagogue, suddenly a man began to display strange behavior. We might call the man a heckler. A heckler is someone who shows up to an event with the intent of causing a disturbance by making noise and interrupting the speaker. That is what the man did when Jesus started to teach in the synagogue. He got ugly and out of order. The man acted up, cried out, yelled, shouted, and interrupted the service with unnecessary remarks. Mark refers to him as having an unclean spirit.

However, Jesus did not have the ruler of the synagogue rush over and put the man out. Instead, Jesus realized that this was not the man, but the demon in the man. Jesus called the demon out of the man and gave the man a new lease on life. Jesus showed compassion for the man. On one occasion, a woman off the streets visited our church while a gospel singing was going on. I am sure that many churches have had its share of visitors such as the woman that decided to look in on us. It never takes long for heads to start turning, noses to start twitching, and eyes to start rolling and for people to start whispering. Just wait awhile and one of the ushers will soon come and say, "Reb, I think you better do something." The woman was "two sheets in the wind." Her clothes were soiled. The woman smelled bad and looked bad. As the choir sang she would jump up and say something. Up and down, up and down, up and down she went fanning the scent everywhere.

Instead of putting the woman out, we managed to get her settled in order that others could enjoy the service. We showed compassion to the woman the same way that Jesus showed compassion for the man. Drawing people to Christ requires compassion. **Compassion is the willingness to identify with someone else's pain, problem and predicament and do something about it. Compassion is the consciousness of others' distress with a desire to alleviate it** [27]

Jesus Demonstrates the Necessity of Prayer

Another lesson learned early on by the disciples was a lesson in the power of prayer. Jesus was tired and weary from ministering to the needs of the crowd. People came from all over to hear Jesus preach. Jesus spent the entire day healing and blessing those in need. He was scheduled to be in another town the following day. However, before Jesus went into the next town he got up early the next morning and spent time in prayer, (Mk.1:35-39). Jews prayed three times a day, morning, noon, and evening. This was most likely the first prayer of the day.

I remember many mornings during a visit to the Holy Lands being awakened from sleep at about five o'clock by the shofar's loud horn blast calling people to prayer.[28] I am not an early riser. I promised that once I got out of the Marines that I would never stand in anyone's long line again and that I would sleep as long as I like. Unfortunately, I still stand in long lines. However, I do sleep in every chance I get. However, I was not as fortunate during the ten day stay in the Holy Lands. Each morning the horn woke us up signaling that it was prayer time.

There is power in prayer. We should take more seriously the teachings of Jesus and start each day with prayer. We should strive to be prayerful throughout the day. However, that does not mean praying out loud and disturbing others. Neither does it mean that we are so engrossed in trying to act spiritual that we accidentally cut off a finger or lose a hand. Prayer can energize us when we are spiritually, physically and emotionally drained. Prayer can empower us for challenges ahead.

Jesus Recognizes Persistence

One other lesson learned early in the life of the disciples was a lesson in forgiveness and persistence. When Jesus returned to Capernaum, people turned out in great numbers to hear him, (Mk. 2:1-12). Among the crowd were four men bent on getting their friend to Jesus. They tried getting in the conventional way but nobody paid them any attention. They tried "excuse me." They tried "may I get by please?" They tried being pleasant and nice. But their good manners failed to get them any closer to Jesus. However, they held it together and did not lose their cool. They demonstrated persistence. When they could not get through the door, and there was no window to climb through and no one would let them through they took the roof off the owner's house. The man's friends demonstrated persistence in the face of opposition. They refused to take "no" for an answer.

Jesus Demonstrates Forgiveness

The man received more than physical healing. The man received forgiveness of his sin. Jesus told the paralytic that his sin had been forgiven. Sin can produce spiritual paralysis. Once the man received forgiveness of his sin he could start fresh. None of us are beyond God's forgiveness. There are people who need to know that they are not beyond forgiveness. Often when people fall into sin, make mistakes and bad choices they feel like the Lord is out to get them, rain on their parade and spoil their party. One of the big discussions we had in a Bible study was the topic of divorce, which we shall share in a later lesson. It was interesting to learn how many believers feel that certain persons are beyond the Lord's compassion and forgiveness. However, Mark teaches us that faith and persistence excites Jesus. He also teaches us that Jesus is compassionate and anxious to forgive.

Jesus demonstrated power everywhere he went. Jesus demonstrated power to show that his authority came from God. He demonstrated power to build the disciples faith in Him. He also demonstrated power to build faith in his disciples.

Lesson Review

1. In what city did Jesus set up his headquarters?

2. What are the two primary regions in Israel?

3. What is a disciple?

4. Discuss the reasons why Jesus demonstrated power.

5. Discuss a time when you had to show persistence.

6. Discuss a time when you had to show compassion.

7. Discuss a time when you had to show forgiveness.

Storm Clouds Rising

And when the scribes and Pharisees saw Him eating with the tax collectors and sinners, they said to His disciples, "How is it that He eats and drinks with tax collectors and sinners (Mk.2:15-16, NKJV)?"

Jesus Calls Matthew

Jesus received a warm welcome to preach and teach in the synagogues before falling out with the religious leaders. However, storm clouds began to rise as time passed and Jesus continued to teach and preach. The religious leaders began to criticize Jesus. They began to whisper and cause a stir among the people. They even tried to get the disciples in the mix of their mess. One such occasion was when Jesus called Matthew to be a disciple. Matthew lived in Capernaum where Jesus had set up his base. It is likely that Matthew got wind of the miracle working preacher before Jesus called him. Matthew was a tax collector. He manned a tax booth in Capernaum. Tax collectors were not the most liked people around. Most people disliked tax collectors because they worked for the Roman government. Since they did not receive wages for their work, they cheated people. They padded the books. They overcharged and robbed people blind. Tax collectors were crooks and trained thieves. Although tax collectors were often wealthy, they were highly disliked.

No doubt, Matthew was in the business where gossip came his way. He got the rumors about Jesus. There were rumors about the four men that took the roof off a house where Jesus was. He heard that Jesus had been along the seashore of Galilee and recruited some fishermen to go with him and preach.

Then one day, Jesus caught Matthew seated at his booth and said to him, "follow me!" Matthew immediately shutdown his booth and followed Jesus. A few days later Matthew threw a party and invited all his tax collector friends over. Tax collectors from all around Galilee showed up. All the hucksters, hustlers, club owners, despised and social outcasts of the city were there. Matthew invited them to tell them that he was not going to be a tax collector anymore. He was going to tell them that he was changing his ways, and turning his life around and going on the road with Jesus. He wanted his friends to meet Jesus. When we leave the life of the world to follow Jesus we should be excited to tell our friends.

Sitting and Eating with Sinners

Imagine what happened when the Pharisees heard that Jesus had called Matthew to be a disciple. They had a problem! When they passed Matthew's place and saw all the beer bottles, poker chips, pool tables, and playing cards and Jesus sitting and eating with them, they lost it. They turned up their noses and started murmuring to each other, "He sits and eats with sinners." They called the disciples over and asked them, "Why does your teacher do this? Why does he sit and eat with sinners? He is supposed to be a preacher. This does not look good." Jesus knows that he is not sitting with the most popular crowd. He knows that he is not rubbing shoulders with the more affluent and cultured crowd. He is sitting among the ones that need him. He is sitting among the ones he came to help.

Jesus put the Pharisees in check when he said to them, "Those that are well do not need a doctor, but sick people do." Jesus was suggesting that the Pharisees needed to be sitting with him along with the other sinners. But they didn't get it. They had no clue. They were unaware of their own spiritual sickness. They were too blind to see that Jesus loves sinners and keeps company with them. He rubs shoulders with those who do not have it all together. He sits and dines with those who are hungry for love and compassion. The religious leaders could not get with the program that Jesus called Matthew to be a disciple. They did not feel as if Matthew fit the bill. A man with a checkered past like Matthew's had no business talking about preaching. This was a mockery and a disgrace. However, Jesus is still calling men and women with a checkered past. He is still calling people like Matthew to leave their tax booths and follow him. Jesus still finds his way to the pool halls, juke joints, bars and dance clubs. He still finds his way into dark allies and smelly streets. He still reaches down in the gutters of life and changes lives. The same way that Jesus saw potential in a low down rascal like Matthew, Jesus sees potential in us.

Jesus and the Disciples Won't Fast

Sitting with sinners was only one of the many issues that the Pharisees had with Jesus. They resented the fact that Jesus and his disciples did not observe all of their self-made traditions. On this occasion they got upset with Jesus because he and his disciples did not fast like everybody else. The Pharisees fasted and John's disciples fasted (Mk. 2:18-20, NKJV). But Jesus and his crew were different. The Mosaic Law prescribed one fast a year, during the Day of Atonement. However, over the years Pharisees added more fasting days. This was a time that they could show-off their piety. They put on sackcloth and painted their faces with ashes and walked around looking sadly religious and holy. When Jesus and the disciples failed to comply they got upset. [29]

An in depth study of the life of Jesus reveals that Jesus intentionally rebelled against the traditions of the religious leaders. He broke rules for the sake of breaking them. He antagonized the Pharisees and Sadducees. Rattled over another blatant act, they asked Jesus why He and his disciples did not follow the rules. Jesus said, "Because I'm here!" "The bride's groom is here. The bride groom is here, Jesus said. This is no time for a funeral. It's feast time! These guys are having the time of their lives. They are preaching the gospel, healing the sick and witnessing miracles in the lives of people. They will fast once the bridegroom is gone."

Jesus was speaking about the days ahead. Jesus told the Pharisees there is no greater pleasure than seeing people coming into the kingdom of God, getting a new lease on life and a fresh start. But the Pharisees did not like it. Jesus referred to them as old wineskins. Sound's kind of like "old hag." Anyway, after talking about the fun the disciples were having Jesus said the reason you can't rejoice is because you are nothing but old wineskins, and you can't put new wine in old wineskins. Everybody listening knew what Jesus was getting at. In short, "If you put new wine in old wineskins the skins would burst.[30]" Jesus accused the Pharisees of being too stiff collared and wound too tightly. Regardless of what Jesus said about them they were not changing. In fact, they were gradually becoming fed up with the way he did things.

Jesus and the Disciples Won't Wash their Hand

One thing after another kept Jesus in trouble with Israel's religious leaders. Rumors about Jesus and the disciple's blatant acts of eating with sinners, refusing to fast and teaching things contrary to the Law of Moses reached all the way to Jerusalem (Mk. 7:1-2) When the religious leaders in Jerusalem heard it they sent representatives down to Galilee to see what was going on and report their findings about the prophet Jesus. Sure enough, they caught Jesus red handed. This time it was an issue over hand washing. Mark takes a moment to clarify the ceremonial hand washing performed by the Jews. Jews and Gentiles shopped at the same market places. They walked the same streets, pushed the same grocery carts and handled some of the same food and cloth items. They brushed against each other in tight places. However, Jews considered Gentiles and Samaritans unclean. They believed that they became defiled and contaminated by being in the same space with Gentiles. No sooner than they got home from the market place they immediately ran to wash their hands.

The spies from Jerusalem witnessed firsthand that Jesus and his disciples did not practice the ceremonial washings. It was not that the Jesus and the disciples did not practice cleanliness and just flopped down to eat without washing their hands. Who wouldn't frown upon anybody that has been working all day and sits down to the table and grabs a piece of chicken with dirty, greasy hands to start eating? However, this was not the case.

Jesus and the disciples did not wash their hands according to the traditions of the religious leaders. They had a prescription for hand washing. Grab your favorite bar of soap Dove, Ivory, Zest, Jergens. It didn't matter what you washed with except it was done the way they said. The ritual prescribed that the hands be held out, palms up, and hands slightly cupped and water poured over them. Then the fist was used to scrub and wash one hand and then the other. The process was repeated. However, this time the hands were stretched out with the palms turned down and water poured over them to wash away the dirty water the defiled hands were washed with. The Pharisees became bitter when they noticed that Jesus and his disciples failed to perform the ceremonial washings as prescribed. Upset over this, the Pharisees from Jerusalem called Jesus on the carpet. "Why don't you and your disciples wash your hands according to the tradition of the elders?" Jesus gave them a quick seminar in biology. He said that nothing entering from the outside can make anyone unclean because it does not go into the heart but the stomach, and then out of the body. Jesus said the heart is where jealousy, meanness, evil, greed, immoral thoughts, slander, arrogance and other dirty thoughts reside. Jesus did not comply with the Pharisees rules for several reasons. Jesus did not accept the oral tradition of the Law. He recognized that the ceremonial washing was a prejudice act aimed at Gentiles and Samaritans. Another reason Jesus did not go along with the Pharisees religious and ceremonial acts is because Pharisees were religious radicals and extremists. The ceremonial washings as they called them were not prescribed by the Law, but prescriptions in addition to the Law. [31] Then too, Jesus did not buy into the religious hypocrisy.

A Desperate Mom

After Jesus finished his short biology seminar, he left Galilee and went into the region of Tyre, where he met a Syrophoencian woman with a pressing problem. **Syro-Phoenicia was the Roman province where the Canaanite woman lived that exercised faith in Jesus to heal her daughter.**[32] Jesus went into a house and gave the disciples specific instructions that he did not want to be disturbed. But the woman showed up and refused to leave until she had seen Jesus. Her daughter was possessed with an evil spirit. Jesus tried to brush the woman off. He told the woman that it was not right to give the children's bread to the dogs. But the woman determined to get what she came for paid no attention to Jesus' "cheap shot." It went right over her head. Too often we allow what people say to rub us the wrong way. Instead of remaining focused on what is really important we sometimes allow ourselves to be discouraged by a sly remark. When Jesus saw that the woman was steadfast in her faith and was not going to leave empty handed, he told her to be at ease because her daughter was healed.

Mark relate the healing of the Gentile woman's daughter with the issues of ceremonial hand washing. Jesus did not only reject the prejudice acts aimed against Gentiles, but he also extended healing to those with faith whether they were Jews or Gentiles. The Syrophoencian woman was desperate. There are desperate moms in the world today that care just as much about their sons and daughters as this woman. However, this mother was also determined. Determination is the deciding factor in so many situations. We must turn our desperation into determination. Determination always wins out.

Pharisees Confront Jesus about Divorce

The religious leaders called Jesus on the carpet on a number of occasions. However, they could never get anything on Jesus. He always escaped their religious traps. Nevertheless, when they saw that they were unsuccessful in trapping him on one religious issue they found something else.

Religious talk is always interesting. Go to the barbershop, the nail shop, and the hair salon. Go hang out at the local corner store or under the tree where the town criers are. Hang around long enough and sooner or later someone is going to bring up something about the Bible. Mind you, most people have very little if any real in sight about the Bible, yet they act as if they are great authoritarians. It is quite unfortunate how people argue and wrangle over the Bible and know very little if anything about the culture and context in which the Bible originated. The interesting thing is most of the barbershop and beauty parlor theology is similar to the Pharisee's conversations with Jesus. The first discussion has not been resolved when someone else chimes in; "Well tell me this, does the Bible . . ." and they are off all over again.

When the Pharisees could not corner Jesus on one thing they jumped to something else. In another attempt to trap Jesus, the Pharisees harped on the issue of divorce. They came and asked Jesus whether it was lawful for a man to divorce his wife (Mk.10:1-12)." Moses permitted a man to divorce his wife by writing a certificate of divorce. Jesus told them that divorce was not in God's sovereign will, but was made possible through God's permissive will, because of hardness of the heart. Jesus answered according to the Law. "If a man divorces his wife and marries another he commits adultery (Deut. 24:1)." By the first century there were two rabbinical schools of thought. Each had their own views about divorce and everything else. Concerning adultery, Rabbi Shammai argued that wife adultery referred to something shameful, or some uncleanness. However, Rabbi Hillel argued that "something shameful or some uncleanness went beyond moral faults to include anything that might be an annoyance or embarrassment to the husband. [33]

Divorce remains to be a touchy topic. People fall on both sides of the argument, Christians included. Some think that divorce is unforgiveable and feel that divorcees are out of fellowship with the Lord. No doubt people have been hurt as a result of divorce. Former spouses are hurt. Children are hurt. Family members on both sides are hurt. Everybody wants to blame somebody else. Needless to say, one person is often more at fault than the other. Someone has been cheating. Someone has been irresponsible. Someone has been abusive. Someone has betrayed trust. These things are hurtful. God would love it if people could get along and live married happily ever after. However, things do not always work out that way. Therefore, God's grace and mercy is available for people that have experienced divorce (Mk. 10:1-9). There is no limit to God's forgiveness. All have sinned and come short! There is healing for divorcees. We should never encourage people to act mean and hostile to one another because marriage did not work out. That is contrary to the teaching of Jesus. Jesus' basic message is about love, forgiveness and reconciliation. Unfortunately, these seem to be the most lacking in church and society.

Divorcees can still enjoy the abundant life that Jesus promised. Family, church and society should do all in their power to help divorcees heal. The church is in the healing and forgiving business. The religious leaders were so caught up in tradition that it did not matter that people were being healed. They placed more emphasis on legalism than they did life.

Jesus Confronts Pharisees on Tradition

Another controversy that emerged between Jesus and the religious leaders was the issue of God's commandments over tradition. However, this time it was Jesus who initiated the argument. Jesus charged the religious leaders of being guilty of placing tradition over what God requires. Tradition had taken precedent over God's law. Tradition is when we find a substitute to offer God over what God requires. Jesus sarcastically applauded the religious leaders on the sly way that they got around God's commandment to take care of their elderly parents once they could no longer look after themselves. The Law taught that a Jew was to honor his father and mother. However, many of the Jewish religious leaders found ways to circumvent the Law. They also helped others circumvent the Law that might present a gift to the Temple. They created something like a tax shelter. A smart way to avoid this responsibility was to pronounce something as Corban. **Corban was a sacrifice, gift or offering dedicated to God by the Jews in fulfillment of a vow.**[34] In other words, money that was set aside to attend to ones parents in old age could be declared a Corban. The money could not be given to the parents, but it could still be used for personal gain.[35]

Jesus called the crowd together and refuted the teachings of the Pharisees. First, Jesus taught that there is no substitute for God's commandments. Second, traditions can be more restricting than God's commandments. Third, Jesus pointed out that we can do all the right things, and still not do them for the right reason. Fourth, Jesus made it clear that there is a big difference between the traditions of men and the commandments of God. Fifth, obedience to God comes from a love of God from the heart. Jesus taught that observing external rules did not correct the nature of the heart. Too often we seek to observe external rules with the hope that God is pleased and satisfied. However, external rules can become traditions that replaces what God requires.

Jesus and the Disciples Violate the Sabbath

The religious leaders kept a close eye on Jesus. They were always somewhere watching and waiting for Jesus to do something they did not like. One Sabbath, Jesus and the disciples were passing through the grain fields when their stomachs started growling and they begin to get hungry. They were nowhere near a grocery store or a fast food restaurant. However, the longer they walked the hungrier they got. Some of them started murmuring about being hungry. Soon Jesus and the disciples started pulling some of the grain to eat and knock the growl off. The minute James and John and a couple of the other disciples pulled some grain the Pharisees popped up. Jumping up from hiding in the grain field, brushing themselves off, and picking at sand spurs they scold Jesus and the disciples about pulling grain on the Sabbath.

Jesus knew how to get under their skin. I suspect that Jesus often did things to flush out and irritate the Pharisees and Sadducees. Imagine Jesus spotting the Pharisees and telling the disciples "Hey, guys the Pharisees are looking, let's not do the hand washing thing today." (Mk.7:1-5 NKJV).

The Pharisees did not like the way Jesus did things. They never warmed up to him. They did not like it that he recruited a tax collector to be his disciple. They question his credibility as a prophet of God because he sat and ate with sinners. They resented him calling them hypocrites. They detested the fact that he claimed power to forgive sins. According to the religious leaders of Israel only God had the power to forgive sin. For someone to suggest that they possess power to forgive sin was like making themselves equal to God. Furthermore, it angered the Pharisees that everybody else followed the rules of ceremonial cleansing except for Jesus and his disciples. Not only did Jesus reject their religious traditions, but he also encouraged his disciples to do the same.

The religious leaders became so angry with Jesus over his miracles that they accused him of being in alliance with Satan. When people have done all they can to destroy someone and nothing is working, they will soon say that you are working with the Devil. They called Jesus Beelzebub. **Beelzebub was another name for Devil, the same as Satan. Beelzebub was regarded as the prince of demons.** [36]

My grandmother would call me Beelzebub whenever she got upset with me about something I did. She would say, "you ole Beelzebub!" Likewise, the religious leaders accused Jesus of being in league with Beelzebub. They accused him of being an agent of Satan. They said that Jesus had a demon and was casting out demons and healing the sick by the power of Satan. Jesus laughed and scorned them for being silly. "He suggested that Satan would not work against himself. Satan wants people to be sick and walking around acting crazy. However, Jesus' power to heal and cast out demons was evidence of the arrival of the kingdom of God.

Jesus Predicts the Destruction of the Temple

Jesus constantly rubbed the religious leaders the wrong way. Another controversial statement that upset the religious leaders was remarks Jesus made about the Temple. Jesus and the disciples had been in the Temple. On the way out, one of the disciples began to marvel at the beauty of the Temple. The Temple was the crowning jewel of Jerusalem and one of the finest religious structures in the world. Herod brought in the best stone masons and architects from Phoenicia. The Temple was built of fine cedar from Lebanon, the purest marble and limestone and the finest gold. The Temple courts were surrounded by huge ornate columns and paved with colorful stones and the gates and doors were gilded with fine tapestry.

However, instead of Jesus being impressed and saying, whoa! Jesus looked at the Temple and predicted that one day it would be destroyed, (Mk. 13: 1-2).

Sadducees Query Jesus on the Resurrection

Sadducees were the liberal religious leaders of Israel. They did not buy into all the superstitious beliefs espoused by Pharisees, especially the resurrection. Since they have a common enemy, the Sadducees came to Jesus with another religious question and guess what it was. It was about the resurrection. This was another attempt to trap Jesus (Mk. 12:18-27). They wanted to know what happens if a woman's husband die and when she marries the brother of the former husband he also dies and eventually all seven brothers die and leave no children whose wife she would be in the resurrection.

Most of us want to know what happens in the world to come and perhaps just about fall over in the Bible each time we come across this passage, hoping that we can get some insight about the afterlife.

Jesus answered them in a sly way that they were religious leaders but ignorant of the scriptures. He told them that there would be no marrying in heaven. Jesus said that in heaven we will be spirit beings like the angels (Mk. 12: 24-25). Jesus also set the Sadducees straight about the dead, that God is the God of the living and not the dead. Seeing that Jesus had survived their query another scribe listening nearby chimed in, "What is the greatest commandment?" The scribe was astonished at Jesus' response. Jesus was also amazed with the man. He encouraged him that he was not far from the kingdom. According to Mark, this ended the questioning for the day (Mk. 12: 34). The Pharisees and Sadducees had to regroup seeing that they had failed at tripping Jesus up.

The Big Problem with Jesus

The religious leader's main issue with Jesus was not that he taught in the synagogue, healed the sick, and performed miracles. But he did it on the Sabbath. The religious leaders of Israel took the Sabbath seriously. The Sabbath was the day that God set aside in the Law of Moses as a day of rest. **The Sabbath was observed from Friday evening to Saturday evening. The Jewish day began at 6:00am and ended at 6:00pm.** [37] The Law said no cooking, no plowing, no carrying, no lifting, and no walking except for a certain distance on the Sabbath. If your ox was in the ditch, you had to wait until the Sabbath was over to get the ox out. I often wonder why Jesus did not just go with the flow and wait until the Sabbath was over. It seems that Jesus had a death wish. To violate ordinances so dear to the hearts of the religious status quo and perform such acts openly on the Sabbath, one could only be looking for trouble.

Mark provides insight regarding the social, religious, and political bones that Jesus picked with the religious leaders. First, Jesus charged the religious leaders with practicing hypocrisy. He said they forsook the commandments of God for religious traditions. Pharisees made the Sabbath burdensome and difficult to keep. They turned the day of rest into a day of religious rigidity. [38] Furthermore, Jesus demonstrates the boldness needed to stand against oppression. Jesus freed himself from the Pharisee's religious bondage and openly rejected traditions that were more harmful than helpful. Jesus also teaches that we should not allow traditions to prohibit us from showing compassion toward people. Unfortunately, the Pharisees and Sadducees failed to see the good Jesus did for looking at the bad and grew weary of him. Although they did not always see eye to eye, both the Pharisees and Sadducees began to see Jesus as a common threat.

The Religious Leader's Controversies with Jesus

Jesus calls Matthew	Mk. 2:13-16
Jesus and the disciples do not fast.	Mk. 2:18-22
Jesus and the disciples pluck corn on the Sabbath.	Mk. 2:23-28
Jesus heals on the Sabbath	Mk. 3:1-6
Jesus and the disciples do not wash their hands.	Mk. 7:1-7
Jesus' view on the issue of divorce.	Mk. 10:1-12
Jesus' view on paying taxes to Caesar	Mk. 12: 13-17
Jesus' view on the resurrection	Mk. 12: 18-27
Jesus and the greatest commandment	Mk. 12: 28-34
Jesus predicts the destruction of the Temple.	Mk. 13:1-2

Lesson Review

1. What was the religious leader's big problem with Jesus?

2. What are some things that Jesus said reside in the heart?

3. What is your view about divorce?

4. Do you think that God deny grace and forgiveness to divorcees?

5. How do feel about divorce?

LESSON 6

The Great Confession

Now Jesus and His disciples went out to the towns of Caesarea Philippi; and on the road He asked His disciples, saying to them, "Who do men say that I am?" So they answered, "John the Baptist; but some say, Elijah; and others, one of the prophets." He said to them, "But who do you say that I am?" Peter answered and said to Him, "You are the Christ." Then He strictly warned them that they should tell no one about Him

(Mk.8:27-30, NKJV).

Biblical scholars identify Jesus' ministry in three stages. The stage of obscurity is when Jesus worked as a carpenter and unknown to the masses. The stage of popularity is when Jesus' preaching spread throughout Israel and people became amazed at his teachings and power to heal. The stage of rejection is when the religious leaders became intolerant to Jesus' teachings and began to conspire to kill him.

Herod's Scandal

The beheading of John the Baptist caused Jesus to begin to move about with caution. One day John the Baptist's preaching got him in trouble when he pointed out the scandal about Herod and Herodias. A scandal is publicized news that can disgrace and discredit someone's reputation. Herod used to go out and hear John the Baptist, (Mk. 6:21). However, one day, John the Baptist said something that Herod did not like. We love the preacher as long as he is talking about somebody else. We love the preacher as long as he is not meddling in our business and stirring in our "Kool-Aid." But let the preacher come down our street and we are ready to find another church.

Herod Antipas took offense to something John the Baptist said in his sermon. Herod was evil, conniving, cunning, and crafty. He became king of Israel through political treachery. The Romans made Herod Antipas', father king. Antipas' daddy Herod the Great was deranged and paranoid. He had his entire family murdered. He had the first born males killed in hopes of killing baby Jesus. Herod the Great had three sons: Archaeleus, Philip and Herod Antipas. On a certain occasion, Herod Antipas went to Rome where his brother Philip and his wife Herodias lived. They took Herod into their home, rolled out the red carpet, gave him the guestroom to enjoy. Herod Antipas and Herodias, Philip's wife started liking each other. They started talking. Talking led to teasing and touching. One day, Herod Antipas caught Herodias at the right moment and seduced her. He divorced his wife and married, his brother, Philip's wife. Sounds like something off Dallas, Scandal or The Have and the Have Nots.

Had Herod Antipas' brother been dead, then the marriage would have been official and acceptable according to Mosaic Law. One day, while he was preaching, John the Baptist told Herod that it was not right to have his brother's wife. Herod had a bitter sweet relationship with John the Baptist, so he threw him in jail, in hopes of scaring John the Baptist. But Herodias never forgot what John the Baptist said. She waited in out.

Herodias planned a big birthday party for Herod Antipas. She arranged that her daughter, Salome would dance for Herod and his guest. All of his high officials were there. Military commanders were there. The leading men from Galilee were there. Herodias daughter, Salome, put on a show. She put on the ritz. She danced from table to table showing here vivacious curves. Her stunning beauty aroused the audience as she danced to Tina Turner's 'Private Dancer and Donna Summer's Bad Girls to use your imagination. The girl's performance was over the top. Drunk, intoxicated, and caught up in the moment, Herod told her to ask for whatever she wanted. He promised that he would even give her a portion of his kingdom. Herodias told her to ask for the head of John the Baptist. Her request knocked Herod off his feet. But he had made a promise and everybody heard it . . . His pride wouldn't let him back out. We should be careful of the promises we make. Many people make promises knowing they can't keep them. Others make promises knowing they are irrational. People make promises knowing that they can be disastrous. Many of us are just like Herod too prideful to come clean. Herod allowed his pride to carry him down the path of no return. So he had John the Baptist's head cut off and brought to Herodias on a silver platter.

When word reached Jesus he and the disciple retreated into the wilderness where he was followed by a large number of people. Jesus popularity spread among the people. The people saw him as a breath of fresh air. He taught with authority. He showed compassion. He healed their sick friends and family members. The crowd followed Jesus and the disciples wherever they went. Jesus decided to get away for a while. It was time for him to find out what his disciples were thinking.

The Leaven of the Pharisees

First, Jesus pulled the disciples aside and told them to beware of the leaven of the Pharisees and Herod. **Leaven is an agent like yeast that causes dough to rise.**[39] Leaven was produced by storing a piece of dough from the previous week and adding juices to promote fermentation. However, if the leaven became infected with bacteria it could get into the whole loaf and make you sick. When Jesus told the disciples to beware of leaven, Jesus was speaking of the misguided teachings of the Pharisees.

I Once was Blind: Jesus Heals a Blind Man

To stress his point, Jesus healed a blind man in Bethsaida. The man was "blind as a bat," when he "bumped" into Jesus. The man could not see a thing. Jesus led the man out of the town. Then Jesus spit in his hands and took the spit and placed it on the man's eyes. Jesus then asked the man, "Do you see anything?" At first, the man said, 'I see men that look like trees." Jesus touched the man again. Jesus kept touching the man until he could see clearly. The healing of the blind man was connected to the Pharisee's bout with Jesus and Jesus' warning to the disciples. Mark suggests that the religious leaders were spiritually blind and beyond healing, whereas the more time the blind man spent with Jesus and the more he was touched by Jesus the better he could see. After the man regained his sight Jesus encouraged him to avoid bad company (Mk.8:22-26). What a wonderful illustration!

Many of us were just like the man in Bethsaida. We ended up with the wrong crowd, in the wrong town, the wrong place and spiritually blind. However, the more we walked with Jesus and Jesus walks with us the better we see. We can see new possibilities. We can see new opportunities. Jesus says the same thing to us that he said to the blind man. Stay out of bad company. Bad company can lead us back into darkness. Bad company can lead us back into the wrong environment. The same day that the man regained his physical sight, Peter's eyes were open to the spiritual identity of Jesus.

A Confession at Caesarea Philippi

After the healing of the blind man in Bethsaida, Jesus and the disciples took a trip to Caesarea Philippi to get away from the growing tensions, the religious feuds, the heated debates and knit-picking religious leaders. Caesarea Philippi is located about 25 miles from Galilee. Caesarea Philippi is a place of splendor and breath taking beauty and a religious Mecca. Herod the Great had a beautiful temple of marble erected in Caesarea Philippi. The Pantheon was there, another gorgeous temple erected to Pan the Greek god. Images of Roman deities were there. The name is a "combo" of Caesar and Philipp. Caesar is the title for the emperor of Rome. Philip was one of King Herod the Great sons. Upon the death of Herod the Great his kingdom was divided into four parts. Philipp was made tetrarch (meaning a quarter) of a portion of his father's kingdom. Philipp made the region a pet project and beautified it to stroke Caesar's ego. Therefore, the region became known as Caesarea Philippi. [40]

When Jesus and the disciples got to Caesarea Philippi, Jesus hit the disciples with a pop quiz. "Who do men say that I am?" The first question is concerning the rumors about Jesus. People were talking all around town. The disciples had been with Jesus for some time. They had seen him in action. They had followed him up and down the dusty roads of Israel for more than two years. They heard his teachings. They witnessed the power of his touch. They worked with him day in and day out. Surely they had heard something. The disciples started looking around, wondering who was going to respond first. Blundering and looking for responses, they said, Elijah, Isaiah, Jeremiah, or one of the prophets. Then Jesus asked them a more personal question. "Who do you say that I am?" There are many opinions out about Jesus. Some say that Jesus was a good man. Some say he was a great prophet. Others say he was just another religious leader. It is important that the believer know who Jesus is. In a world of hurt, hunger and hatred it is important to know who Jesus is. In a world that is constantly changing before our eyes it is important to know who Jesus is. In a world of unexpected mishaps it is important to know who Jesus is.

When we are certain about who Jesus is we can speak boldly about Christ the way Peter did. "Peter saved the day, "You are the Christ, the son of the living God!" Peter had been given spiritual sight, (Mk. 8:27-30). Matthew adds, "flesh and blood did not reveal this . . . (Matt. 16:16-17). However, the greatest confession is not only in saying who Jesus is, but doing what Jesus did and following in his footsteps. Again, Jesus told the disciples not to broadcast his identity, (Mk.1:40-45; 8:26, 30-see the lesson on the Messianic Secret).

After Peter's confession Jesus began to equip the disciples for the tragedy ahead. For the first time he told them that he was going to suffer and be rejected by the religious leaders of Israel and killed, (Mk.8:31-38). According to Mark, this signified a turn in Jesus ministry. When Peter first met Jesus he was reluctant to carry his boat out in the deep and cast his net after an unsuccessful night of fishing. Peter had even told Jesus to stay away from him and not get to close him. However, as time passed Peter became endeared to Jesus. Die! You are going to die! Peter scolded Jesus and told him not to talk like that. The last thing Peter wanted to hear was that Jesus was going to be taken away, not to mention being killed. Jesus rebuked Peter, and called him Satan. Step back and be quiet, Jesus said! A few minutes earlier Peter was the star student.

Even in our deepest revelation and relationship with God, we are still subject to human frailty and lack the vision to see what God sees. Jesus had called the disciples to be fishers of men, but the mission was becoming more perilous. Seeing the end from a distance Jesus said to the disciples "If any man desires to follow me, let him take up his cross and follow me, (Mk. 8:34)."

Excitement on the Mountain

Six days after Peter's great confession in Caesarea Philippi, Jesus carried Peter, James and John with him where he was transfigured on a mountain. Biblical scholars believe that this event took place on Mt. Hermon. This place became known as the Mount of Transfiguration. We had an opportunity go up on the Mount of Transfiguration during the visit to the Holy Land. The view was breath taking. I imagined the conversation that took place between Moses, Elijah and Jesus. I could hear Peter in the background. During Jesus transfiguration on the mountain, God put on another special effects show. Elijah and Moses appeared on the mountain and talked to Jesus. None of the gospel writers shared what was said. However, I suspect that Moses and Elijah may have given Jesus some encouraging words. Perhaps they told him that they had been waiting for this moment a long time. Perhaps they told him the importance of not turning back. Perhaps they told him that the mission he was about to complete held the destiny of the human race. Elijah represented the prophets. Moses represented the Law. Jesus is the fulfillment of the law and prophets.

Peter, James and John were eye witnesses to Jesus' transfiguration. Afraid and excited at the same time, Peter interrupted the conversation to ask Jesus if they could chill on the mountain for a moment. "Let us build three tents." There is something about being in the presence of the Lord that makes you want to stay all day, even though there is work in the valley. Have you ever had church so good that even after the benediction was given the lights were turned out and the doors were locked, but everybody is still hanging around? I'm talking about somebody prayed like they really know the Lord. The choir sounded good. The ushers were in step, and the preacher preached. After the service was over nobody was anxious about leaving. That's having church! That's what happened on the mountain where Jesus was transfigured. Nobody wanted to leave. Peter said, "It is good to be here."

An Embarrassing Moment

Even as the disciples were celebrating on the mountain, there was work that demanded their presence in the valley. A man in the valley was in desperate need of help. His son was a danger to himself and everybody around him. The man's son constantly tried to destroy himself. Jesus had left some of the disciples in the valley just in case someone came looking for him. Jesus had empowered the disciples to do what he did; heal the sick, cast out demons and give sight to the blind. When the man saw Jesus' disciples he immediately ran to where they were. Standing behind his son, the man explained the symptoms to the disciples. I am certain that the disciples gave it their best effort. They told the boy, "Put your hands up and say "Jesus, Jesus, Jesus," but nothing happened. They called for the oil and anointed the boy, but nothing happened. They went through all their antics and rituals, but they were powerless to do anything about the boy's problem."

Jesus sent the disciples forth to heal the sick and cast out demons, but they were not able to do it. What an embarrassing situation! While the disciples down the mountain are running around like chickens with their heads cut-off, Peter is basking in the excitement on the mountain. God quickly nipped Peter's thought in the bud. "This is my beloved Son, said the voice from Heaven." As they came down from the mountain Jesus told them to be quiet until he was arisen from the dead. This is the second time that Mark has called our attention to Jesus' fate. "He commanded them to tell no one the things they had seen, till the Son of Man had risen from the dead, (Mk. 9:1-10)"

The boy's father was frustrated and out done that the disciples of Jesus were not able to help him. Suddenly, the man with the demon possessed son caught a glimpse of Jesus and the other disciples coming from the mountain. He immediately ran to Jesus and reported his disappointment. "I brought him to your disciples, but they were not able to cast the demon out." Here is one of those times that Jesus scolded the disciples. "O You of little faith!" The disciples often irritated Jesus because of their lack of faith. Jesus told them to bring the boy to him. Jesus healed the man's son and told the disciples that they needed to spend more time fasting and praying and less time fraternizing with the crowd.

We should strive to make sure that we are not an embarrassment to Jesus. Bishop Webster once preached 'Going Up to Come Down!" We have distorted the meaning of going to church. Most people go to church to benefit themselves. They attend to feel good about themselves and in some way hopefully stroke God's ego. We should attend church in order that we can become better students of the Word, better people, better parents and better citizens. However, worship should empower us to help others. One church had the slogan, "We Gather to Worship and Depart to Serve." Bishop Jackson says, the "the church scattered is more effective than the church gathered." In other words, our mountain top experiences should empower us for the work in the world. Jesus told the disciples that the reason they were unsuccessful in casting the demon out of the boy was because they lacked spiritual power. It is interesting to note that Peter, James and John always seemed to stay close to Jesus. However, the other disciples in many instances seemed to be often absent. Perhaps they did not spend as much time with Jesus. The more time we spend with Jesus the more effective we are in life and in ministry.

Jesus Visits Gentile Country

The Gospel of Mark focuses upon Jesus' ministry in Galilee. Chapters one through six is a running record of Jesus' teachings and miracles in Galilee. However, Jesus did not spend all of his time in Galilee. In Mark 1:38, Jesus told the disciples that there were other places and people that needed to hear the gospel. The Gospel recorded by John provides insight into Jesus' ministry in Judea. As Jesus' ministry began to come to an end we see Jesus visiting towns that were occupied by Gentiles. This region was referred to as Galilee of the Gentiles or Decapolis**. Decapolis was ten cities (ten-deka, Grk, polis-city) built by the Romans around 63BC, settled by the Greeks and the practice of Greek culture.** [41]

Chapters six through nine give a brief account of Jesus' ministry in Decapolis. Gennesaret, Tyre, Sidon, the Decapolis, Dalmanutha, and Bethsaida were some of the Gentile towns that Jesus visited. Jesus' ministry in these different regions reveals the distance that Jesus will go to get the word out about the Kingdom of God. Not only is Jesus willing to go the distance, but he is also willing to face the danger.

Jesus Meets a Wild Man

Jesus visited a place called Gadara. **This was the region where the tribe of Gad settled. Gad was one of the twelve sons of Jacob.** [42] While he was there Jesus encountered a man that lived in a graveyard. The story line sounds like something right out of a horror movie. The man lost his direction in life. He began to dibble and dabble in things he knew nothing about. He left his wife and children and started hanging around dead things. He resorted to living in the graveyard.

As kids we learned that the graveyard is no place to hang out. Growing up we heard stories about graveyards. We were told that you could get robbed in the graveyard. We were told that someone might snatch you, kidnap you and even kill you in the graveyard. But this man lived in the graveyard. The People that used to know the man were afraid of him. His family was afraid of him. His friends didn't know him anymore. He terrorized the community. He cut himself with stones. He walked around naked and howled at the moon. People tried to help the man by binding him in chains, but the man broke free of the chains. The man was tormented. We know people that fit the profile of our graveyard wandering friend. They live in torment! They are tormented by life, tormented by lack, tormented by lost and loneliness. So they gave up! They lost their way and started hanging around dead stuff and dead beats. They are no longer the people we used to know. They scare us. The more we try to help them the worst they get.

However, Jesus heard the man's cry from a distance. He heard the man crying and howling in the graveyard. Jesus loaded the disciples in a boat to go where the man was. On their way a storm popped up. The wind and rain pounded down on the boat. But Jesus kept sailing through the dark and danger to get to the man. When Jesus arrived, the man ran out of the graveyard, eyes blood shot, teeth gritting, clothes torn off and broken chains dangling from his wrist. The man called himself Legion. **Legion was the term used by the Romans to define a major military unit in the Roman army. A legion consisted of three thousand to six thousand infantry troops and one hundred to two hundred Calvary troops.**[43] According to Mark, the Gadarene demoniac was possessed with as many demons as one of the Roman's largest military units.

Jesus spoke to the demons and demanded them to come out of the man. When Jesus got done with the man he was clothed in his right mind. The people of Gadara had mixed feelings about the man's recovery and being restored to his right mind. Some of them were amazed. Others were angered. It is interesting how people respond to what happens to other people. One group was elated that the man was back to his old self. They were elated that he was getting his life back on track. They were elated that he would no longer be a terror to the neighborhood. The other group was angered that the man was sitting at the feet of Jesus. They wanted the man to continue walking around acting crazy, howling at the moon and cutting himself. They wanted something to laugh about. That is why they ran Jesus out of town.

Jesus went the distance to get to the man. He sailed through darkness and danger. Jesus could have told the disciples to turnaround. He could have told them the weather was too bad, that the lightning was too vicious and the thundering was too violent. Nevertheless, Jesus weathered the storm and the danger to get to where the man was. Jesus does the same for us. There is no distance or danger that Jesus is not willing to endure to make a difference in the lives of people.

According to Mark, Jesus' visit to Gentile country evidences the inclusiveness of Jesus' message. Jesus' movement from Galilee to the Gentiles suggests God's salvation was available to all people. Gentiles being persecuted in the Roman Empire no doubt rejoiced at Mark's report. Their faith would be strengthened knowing that Jesus had visited many of their Gentile cities as he travelled through Israel preaching and healing.

Lesson Review

1. Who does the blind man in the story represent?

2. Discuss the disadvantages of blindness.

3. Compare physical blindness with spiritual blindness

4. Discuss someone you know who lives in a spiritual graveyard.

5. Discuss someone you know similar to the man in the story.

Chasing Greatness

Now as He was going out on the road, one came running, knelt before Him, and asked Him, "Good Teacher, what shall I do that I may inherit eternal life?" So Jesus said to him, "Why do you call me good? No one is good but One, that is, God. You know the commandments: 'Do not commit adultery,' 'Do not murder,' 'Do not steal,' 'Do not bear false witness,' 'Do not defraud,' 'Honor your father and your mother.' And he answered and said to Him, "Teacher, all these things I have kept from my youth." Then Jesus, looking at him, loved him, and said to him, "One thing you lack: Go your way, sell whatever you have and give to the poor, and you will have treasure in heaven; and come, take up the cross, and follow Me." But he was sad at this word, and went away sorrowful, for he had great possessions

(Mk.10:17-22, NKJV).

Jesus Loves the Little Children

On the way, to another preaching engagement, Mark allows us to catch a glimpse of Jesus' human side as he took a moment with kids. Too often we miss the point that Jesus was just as human as he was divine. However, Jesus got tired, sleepy, thirsty and hungry. Jesus had a social life. He attended weddings and Jewish festivals. He even took time to play with children. The same way that people brought friends and family members for Jesus to heal, parents brought their children for Jesus to bless. The children crowded around Jesus. They climbed into his lap. They played in his hair. They rubbed his face, and pulled at his beard. "Is that real one of them asked?" "Do a miracle for us, chimed another." "Are you going to make some more Kool-Aid, asked another?" "My daddy said you were at a wedding when the wine ran out."

Knowing that Jesus had much work to do and lots of people to heal parents were always trying to pull their children out of the way. Step back! Jesus is preaching. Even the disciples tried to run the children off. But Jesus said, "Let the children come to me." Nobody can beat Jesus kissing babies. He is a master at it. Jesus loves children. We should teach children to love Jesus and to love like Jesus.

Jesus Meets Richie Rich

After a moment with the kids Jesus headed out. A young man caught a glimpse of him getting away and ran him down. This is the story of the "The Rich, Young Ruler. All three of the synoptic gospel writers tell the story of this young man. This began Jesus' teaching on greatness. Breathing hard, panting, trying to catch his breath and talk at the same time, the man fell on his knees at the feet of Jesus. He had a pressing concern. Looking up at Jesus he asked, "Good teacher, what must I do to inherit eternal life?" At first sight we are compelled to applaud the young man. First, he came to Jesus. He was talking to the right person and asking the right question. During the three years of Jesus' preaching and teaching, no one had ever asked this question. The young man wanted to know what he needed to do get to heaven. Believe it or not that still remains to be a very important question. Jesus responded according to the Law. Do not murder. Do not commit adultery. Do be a false witness. You know the commandments, Jesus said. Jesus stressed to the rich young ruler the need to be a moral and upright citizen. Jesus could hardly finish before the young man blurted, "I've got that. I have not stolen anything. I have not killed anyone. I love my parents. I am not a liar. Since I am rich and have everything, I have no need to be jealous of anyone. I have done all these things since I was a boy." The young man made it a point to stress to Jesus how good he was. Many people think that they will get to heaven by being good. They think that Jesus is going to add up everything that they have done and hope that their good will outweigh their bad. We should be good citizens and do good deeds. Unfortunately, being good does not merit salvation. We are saved by grace through faith. However, we should do good works because we are saved.

Now, Jesus had dropped the rich young ruler a hint before he got started. "Why do you call me good? No one is good except God." But the rich young ruler missed it. So Jesus said, Ok! Sell what you have, give it to the poor, and follow me." When Jesus told the man this he shed light on how good the man really was. It turned out that the rich young ruler was covetous. He had not kept the Law as perfectly as he had thought. He loved his money. Money was his god. "Sell everything," Jesus said. The young man had heard enough. He left sad because what Jesus told him to do was too much to ask.

Jesus pointed out to the disciples how difficult it is for rich people to enter the kingdom of Heaven. Jesus did not condemn wealth. He simply showed how wealth can give a false sense of security. "He went away sad, because he had great wealth, (Mk.10:22)." The rich young ruler like so many people felt secure in the Law. "I don't hurt anybody." "I don't bother anybody." "I'm a good person." "I do everything right". The rich young ruler thought that eternal life was in keeping the Law and doing everything right. He was too secure in his wealth to give it up. He did not realize that wealth was not for hoarding, but for helping others. Jesus showed the rich young ruler that serving others opens the door to eternal life and greatness.

Reserved Seats

James and John must not have been around to hear Jesus' conversation with the rich young ruler. If they were it went in one ear and out the other. The disciples were also in pursuit of their own greatness. As they were traveling, Jesus over heard them arguing about who was going to be the greatest. The disciples had seen enough hanging with Jesus to begin jockeying for positions. But they were slow to understand. Everything Jesus said seemed to go over the disciple's head. Jesus had mentioned dying three times and the disciples still did not get it. No sooner than Jesus was done talking to the rich young ruler, James and John slipped off from the other disciples, went to Jesus and put their bid on the table. "Grant us to sit one on your right hand and the other on your left, in your glory." After all, Jesus was "kinfolk." Mary and Salome were sisters. Mary was the mother of Jesus. Salome was the mother of Zebedee's two sons, James and John. Elizabeth the mother of John the Baptist was also Mary's cousin, (Mk. 15:40, Jn.19:25). Jesus, John the Baptist, along with James and John were cousins. They shared the same house. They played together, shared the same room, ate at the same table and wore each other clothes. They knew that "Cuz" had their backs and would give them special positions and special privileges. The disciples had a twisted view of greatness. They thought greatness was looking important. They thought greatness was being dressed up. They thought greatness was being first, being out front, calling the shots and telling other people what to do, (Mk. 10:35-45). The disciples had big ambitions and James and John made theirs known to Jesus. They made the right choice even though they didn't have the right motive. They wanted to be big shots. However, they had no sense of cost. They had no sense of sacrifice. They had no sense of suffering and all that comes with greatness. Jesus had just told the rich young ruler to sell all that he had and follow him, but the disciples missed the point.

However, Jesus did not put down their ambitions, but he quickly put their ambitions in check and got a handle on their twisted thinking. Jesus asked them if they could handle the request they were making. He asked if they were willing to make the sacrifice to lay hands on their request. There is a reality show called The Biggest Loser that helps us understand Jesus' point. The Biggest Loser is about people winning through losing, and gaining by giving up something.[44] Many people want more power, more authority, more position, more this and more that but not at the expense of sacrifice. Some people want better homes, better cars and better credit, but not at the expense of paying their bills on time. Some people want better health, but not at the expense of exercising and eating properly. Some people want better jobs, but not at the expense of more school and more training.

The rich young ruler left sad because of what he had to give up. He and the disciples desired greatness but not at such a high cost. We too may be attached to something that is hard to give up. However, if we are seeking greatness we should be prepared to give up something. We should be prepared to serve, prepared to make a sacrifice and prepared to put others first. However, Jesus promises that in the end the biggest loser becomes the biggest winner (Mk. 10:29-31).

Lesson Review

1. What is ambition?

2. What caused the young man's sadness?

3. Discuss an ambition you may have.

4. Discuss something you have had to give up for your ambition.

5. Discuss how your ambition will serve other.

6. What are some things we should do if we desire to be great?

The Straw that Broke the Camel Back

Now the next day, when they had come out from Bethany, He was hungry. And seeing from afar a fig tree having leaves, He went to see if perhaps He would find something on it. When He came to it, He found nothing but leaves, for it was not the season for figs. In response Jesus said to it, "Let no one eat fruit from you ever again." And His disciples heard it. So they came to Jerusalem. Then Jesus went into the temple and began to drive out those who bought and sold in the temple, and overturned the tables of the money changers and the seats of those who sold doves. And He would not allow anyone to carry wares through the temple. Then He taught, saying to them, "Is it not written, 'My house shall be called a house of prayer for all nations'? But you have made it a 'den of thieves.' And the scribes and chief priests heard it and sought how they might destroy Him; for they feared Him, because all the people were astonished at His teaching. When evening had come, He went out of the city.

(Mk. 11:12-19, NKJV).

Jesus and the Disciples Head for Jerusalem

Most of us have heard the phrase, "The straw that broke the camel's back." It is an Arabic proverb that defines a series of events that lead to disaster. All of us have a stopping point and a push beyond that point can cause trouble. According to Mark, the religious leaders of Israel labeled Jesus as a radical revolutionist and a menace to the Law. Jesus' continuous refusal to abide by their traditions and follow their rules put them on edge. Jesus was also growing tired of the Pharisee's and Sadducee's hypocrisy and self righteous ways. One more act could push everybody over the edge.

According to Mark, the series of events that took place during the week of Passover created an irreconcilable friction between Jesus and the religious leaders. The Christian community refers to this week as Passion Week. Passion Week starts with Jesus' entry into Jerusalem and ends with Jesus' resurrection.

Jesus' ministry carried him and the disciples back and forth between Galilee and Judea. However, Mark sheds very little light on Jesus' ministry in Judea. The Gospel of John gives us a better picture. Once again, Jesus and the disciples left Galilee and went into Judea. Jesus had spoken about being put to death on at least two other occasions. On the way to Jerusalem to observe the Passover, Jesus decided to make another announcement about the matter of dying.

Jesus was followed by a great crowd. Many of those that he healed were in the crowd. The woman with the issue of blood was in the crowd. Jairus and his daughter were in the crowd. Peter's mother-in-law was in the crowd. If Jesus has done anything for us we should be somewhere in the crowd. As they were walking and talking they came near the city of Jericho. Jericho was about eighteen miles northeast of Jerusalem. Jericho was a beautiful city. Herod the Great had launched a beautification campaign for the entire city. He had palm trees planted throughout the city so that Jericho was called the "City of Palms".

Blind Bartimaeus Sees Jesus

On the outskirts of Jericho, Jesus was interrupted by a blind beggar name Bartimaeus. It was customary for the blind, the poor and the lame, to sit and beg for money from people that were passing. The crowd tried to silence the blind man. But the blind man kept calling Jesus until Jesus stopped and responded to the blind man's need, (Mk.10:46-52).

Mark began to draw the curtains close to Jesus' ministry with the healing of the blind man. According to Mark, this was the last miracle performed by Jesus. Unlike the Pharisees and Sadducees who were spiritually blind and had no desire to see, "Blind Bartimaeus cried out to Jesus for help. He wanted to see! Bartimaeus was tired of walking in darkness and being led around by other people. When Jesus heard Bartimaeus' cry, he stood still and called the blind man and restored his sight. When Bartimaeus received his sight he followed Jesus in the way. No doubt Bartimaeus had a lot of catching up to do with his friends, family and people that he knew. He could have chosen many other places to go, McDonalds, Happy Hour, or the hottest happenings in town, but he followed Jesus.

Too often people that have been blessed by the Lord go in the opposite direction. They get spiritual amnesia. All the promises about if only the Lord will help me, deliver me, heal me, save my child, save my family and let me win the lottery goes out the window. They soon find their old friends and their old place in life. This was not the case with Bartimaeus. He followed Jesus in the way. The greatest way to express our gratitude for the Lord's grace and mercy is to follow him in the way.

Hail King Jesus

When Jesus and the disciples and the crowd reached the city of Bethphage, Jesus sent two of them into town (Mk.11:1) Bethphage was east of Jerusalem and was situated so that it provided a magnificent overhead view of the Holy City and the Temple. Jesus had spoken to a man in the town and made arrangements to borrow a colt so that he could ride into the city of Jerusalem. When the people heard that Jesus was coming they got so excited that they staged a parade. People lined the streets to see him. They spread their coats and outer garments in the streets. They broke palm branches and threw them in the streets. They cheered and shouted, "Hosanna, Hosanna, blessed is he who comes in the name of the Lord." **This event is celebrated in the Christian community as Palm Sunday. Many Christians relive Palm Sunday by spreading palm branches and wearing palm leaves. This event is also called, Jesus' triumphant entry into Jerusalem.** [45]

However, this was no triumphant entry for the religious leaders. You can imagine what the religious leaders did when they read the local news headlines: "The Prophet Jesus of Nazareth to Visit Jerusalem." "Jesus Rides into the Holy City." "The Prophet Jesus Hailed King by the Town People." Jesus' ride into Jerusalem and the people's shouts of hosanna stirred the religious leaders against Jesus even more. They did not like it that the common people liked Jesus and wanted him to be their king. This struck a nerve. This was getting to be too much.

Jesus Walks through the Temple

Jesus rode into Jerusalem, walked into the Temple, looked around and walked out. Jesus did not bother to stay for the service. Jesus didn't even hang around to catch the sermon. Some people do not care to spend much time in church; however, they do try to arrive there in time for the preaching. Most preachers attending revivals will call and ask the host pastor, "What time the preacher getting up, Doc?" But Jesus was not even interested in hearing the sermon. It didn't matter whether the preacher had three points, a whoop or a holler. Jesus went right back out the door. Jesus saw something that turned him off. He saw something that disgusted and frustrated him. I wonder whether or not Jesus has ever stopped by our churches and walked out because of something he saw. He saw tipping but no tithing. He saw people but no power. He saw politics but no praise. He saw money but no mercy. Whatever Jesus saw did not let him rest well. He got no sleep that night. Jesus couldn't wait to get up the next morning.

Waking up to a Bad Day

Jesus awakened the disciples and told them to get up and get dressed. Jesus did not bother to have his morning cup of coffee, work the crossword puzzle, and read the news. He skipped breakfast and headed straight for the Temple. It was evident that Jesus was going to have a bad day. Have you ever gotten up in the morning and knew by the way things started-off that you were going to have a bad day? There's no soap, no tooth paste, you can't find your keys, nothing matches, you're running late and everybody is moving slow as snails. You know you are in for a bad day. More and more I am learning to watch the red flags that says, "Slow down and pray, it's going to be one of those days."

On the way back into Jerusalem Jesus got hungry. As they were walking he caught a glimpse of a fig tree from a distance. Jesus was certain that he would find some figs on the tree to hold him until lunch. However, when he got to where the fig tree was there were leaves but no figs. Jesus lost his cool and cursed the fig tree (Mk.11:12-14). This may appear to have been cruel of Jesus to curse an innocent fig tree. However, Mark suggests that Jesus' action against the fig tree revealed the state of the religious leaders of Israel. As leaders and rulers of God's chosen people they were spiritually blind and fruitless. They were like the fig tree with leaves but no fruit. The religious leaders gave the appearance of being religious. They gave the appearance of being fruitful. They gave the appearance of being holy and pious walking around in their long flowing robes.

Jesus Wrecks the House

The Passover was at hand. The Passover commemorated the Jews exodus from Egypt under the leadership of Moses. A lamb was sacrificed and eaten to remember the night that God slaughtered the first born of Egypt. The food consisted of lamb, unleavened bread, and bitter herbs. People from all over the Roman Empire poured into Jerusalem for the Passover. Jews, proselytes, merchants, sailors, businessmen, wayfarers and sojourners came to Jerusalem. They came to worship God. They came to offer sacrifices. They came to have a good time. Booths were scattered throughout the streets. The Passover was a time of festivity. More than five hundred thousand people were in the city at Passover.

A garrison of Roman soldiers was housed in the Fortress of Antonia, near the Court of the Gentiles. Roman soldiers patrolled the streets and were posted on every corner to keep the peace. But that did not matter to Jesus. As they drew closer to Jerusalem Jesus began to break-off tree limbs and plait them together. Jesus shook and swung the switch to make sure it was sturdy and durable. When Jesus arrived at the Temple he didn't ask any questions, he just started cutting. Parents use to say, "If I have to come in there one more time I'm not asking any questions. I'm coming in cutting right and left." That is what Jesus did. He went into the Temple and turned over the money changing booths. He drove the animals out. He attacked the religious leaders and beat them out of the Temple. Jesus took all the money and slung it everywhere, shouting, "My house should be called a house of prayer but you have made it a den of thieves." Jesus wrecked the place. There was not a table or chair left standing. The money boxes were all shattered, cracked, broken and busted up. The religious leaders edgy, shaking, looking over their shoulder afraid of getting hit again crawled around trying to gather the money. Jesus was angered at the way the religious leaders had corrupt the house of God. This was the final straw! They cheated people that came to present their sacrifices to the priests. They found defects in the animals that the people brought to the Temple. They made them buy their doves, pigeons, and sheep at inflated prices. They charged high interest to change money. There were so many animals in the Temple that there was no room for people to worship. Jesus swept the house and ran everybody out. John gives a more detailed account of the event, (Jn. 2:13-17).

This was also the final straw with the religious leaders of Israel. Jesus had pushed the Pharisees and Sadducees to their limit. He had overstepped his bounds. When the religious leaders got the news about what happened they were determined to make Jesus pay. They had tolerated his Sabbath healings, his violations of ceremonial washings, and his controversial teachings in the synagogue. But this was too much.

Either Jesus was having a bad day, deranged, death struck or divinely driven. What Jesus did was sure to get him in hot water with the religious leaders. He road into Jerusalem and offered himself as the Messiah knowing that this would not set well. He allowed the people to announce him as a king, when Herod was king. He then went in and wrecked the Temple and threw the money everywhere. Most people will let you get away with almost anything. Just don't bother the money. Both Jesus and the religious leaders had had enough. The religious leaders had reached their limit. Jesus had reached his limit. What Jesus saw in the Temple was the final straw. What Jesus did to the Temple and the religious leader's money was the final straw.

Enough is Enough

As soon as Jesus and the disciples left the Temple, the news spread like wildfire about what happened in the Temple. It did not take long for word to get back to the Sadducees about the mess Jesus made. The Sadducees reported the news to the Pharisees. Jesus did not run and hide after wrecking the Temple. Instead, He and the disciples showed-up in the Temple as if nothing had happened. It was obvious that something had to be done about Jesus. The chief priests, the elders, and the teachers of the Law found Jesus walking around in the Temple and asked him why he wrecked the Temple. "You have disrespected us and embarrassed us." The people are watching and we can't afford to have you challenging our authority." "Who sent you?" "Who are you working for?" "Who gave you authority to come in here and run everybody out and tear up everything and throw money around?" We have overseen this Temple for years, long before you were born." "We know your people, knew your daddy, Joseph, well." "He was a good carpenter." We know your mama, Mary. We also know your cousin's James and John's people, Zebedee and Salome. Your mama Mary and Elizabeth are also cousins. She was an old lady when she had her first son. Another of the religious leaders added, "Yeah, her boy had a death wish, John the Baptist!" "Herod cut off his head for preaching all that crazy stuff." "That was your cousin, wasn't it?" "It looks like you are going to end up the same way." Help us to understand why you speak against Moses, heal on the Sabbath and wrecked the Temple. "You could be an asset to your people if you would conform to the system."

Driven by Divine Passion

Jesus did not bother to dignify the Pharisees and Sadducees with an answer. They were beyond reform. They had become big headed and power hungry. The money was coming in too good. They were in control. It requires the kind of courage and boldness that

Jesus showed in the Temple to get the oppressor's attention. This is not the happy go lucky, turn your cheek, give up the right for the wrong and go the extra mile Jesus we see in Matthew (Matt.5). Doctrinally and theologically Christians believe that Jesus is the Son of God that came to die to take away the sins of the world, and restore humankind to a right relationship with God. But let's be frank! Jesus risked being put to death by breaking the rules and rituals established by the Law and the traditions of the religious leaders. Jesus knowingly went against the grain and even pressed his disciples to follow suit. Jesus brought his life to an early end because he was a radical, a revolutionist, and a non-conformist driven by divine passion to do something about corruption. He was divinely driven to stand for justice and righteousness. He was divinely driven to be the voice for the oppressed. It is difficult to keep silent when you are driven by divine persuasion to stand against oppression. You are bound to upset someone. There is no turning back once the die is cast.

When Martin Luther nailed his ninety-five thesis to doors of Wittenburg Catholic Church and the Catholic Church demanded him to recant, Martin Luther said, "Hear I stand, I can do no other." When whites and blacks encouraged Dr. Martin King to wait and be silent, King declared in his letter from the Birmingham jail, I can't wait. He declared I am here because injustice is here. He went on to say that injustice anywhere is a threat to justice everywhere. Malcolm X, Mahatni Ghandi, Nelson Mandela and others followed the footsteps of Jesus the revolutionist.

Too often we see the corruption in the work place, in government, as well as in the church and do nothing. We see greed and oppression at work and do nothing. We see innocent people hurt and their faith destroyed and do nothing. We see religious politics and religious oppression at work and do nothing. Unfortunately, very few people are divinely driven. Such boldness comes at a great price and at a cost most of us are not willing to pay. Subsequently, divine passion can get you crucified.

Instead of answering their question on his authority, Jesus asked them about his cousin John the Baptist. "Was John the Baptist sent from God or did he start preaching on his own?" They knew Jesus had cornered them. They were in a no win situation. It irked them even when they showed up in the Temple the next time and caught Jesus telling a parable that was about them (Mk.12:1-11). They wanted Jesus off the streets. Perhaps if they could get him off the streets the commotion would die down. Things would quiet down. They felt that they could regain control and get back to business as usual. They hesitated to arrest Jesus for fear of causing a riot. The people loved Jesus. However, they continued to work behind the scene, seeking ways to trap Jesus that they may bring charges against him. A group of Pharisees and Herodians (Sadducees) joined together to catch Jesus in a trap (Mk.12:13-17). It has been mentioned before that these two did not always get along. Pharisees and Sadducees refuted each other over religious issues. Pharisees believed in angels and spirit beings, Sadducees did not. Pharisees believed in Mosaic Law and oral tradition. Sadducees only accepted the written Law of Moses. Pharisees were conservative and Sadducees were liberals. Satan knows how to bring your enemies together. He is masterful at finding people who enjoy evil to serve his purpose.

Another Trap

Jesus had stepped on the toes of Israel's two most powerful religious factions, the Pharisees and Sadducees. They were not going to take it lying down. One day during the Passover after the episode in the Temple, the Pharisees came to stroke Jesus' ego. They told Jesus what an inspiration he was. They commended him that he stood his ground and was not persuaded by men. "You teach the word of God truthfully," they said. Jesus sensed that something was up. Either these guys woke up on the wrong side of the bed, had a fever, or had a radical change overnight. However, Jesus let them speak. After a little ego stroking they pounced upon Jesus with their trick question. "Should we pay taxes to Caesar?" (Mk. 12: 13-17). The Jews resented paying taxes to Rome. The religious leaders resented bringing money into the Temple that had Caesar's image on it. The Law strictly prohibited the making of graven images and the likeness of anything in the earth. Many Jews flat out refused to pay the tax. However, there was not much that they could do, Rome ran everything. So they plotted to get rid of Jesus by getting him to say something against Caesar. However, Jesus was always steps ahead. Jesus said, "Bring me a coin." They looked at each other befuddled over what Jesus was getting ready to do. One of the religious leaders nodded to the other, "Give him a coin." Fumbling and shaking he pulled his robe up and brought out a denarius. **In ancient Rome a denarius was a silver or gold coin equal to a quarter.** [46]

Jesus looked at the coin and displayed a sly smile, knowing they were trying to trap him. "Whose image is on the coin, Jesus asked?" One of them, said, Caesar is on the coin, but what does that have to do with anything?" Jesus gave them a quick lesson on the importance of paying taxes. Give to Caesar what belongs to Caesar and give to God what belongs to God" Jesus made it clear that we should pay our taxes, pay our bills and pay others whatever we owe them. Jesus suggests that that our duty to the state does not infringe upon our duty to the Lord. They thought they had Jesus when they he pulled the old coin trick, but Jesus escaped another one of their traps.

Lesson Review

1. What is the significance of Palm Sunday?

2. Why did Jesus drive out the money changers?

3. Discuss a time you have been pushed to the edge.

4. Discuss a situation where you have witnessed abuse of power.

5. How do you handle authority?

Curtain Call

> *After two days it was the Passover and the Feast of Unleavened Bread. And the chief priests and the scribes sought how they might take Him by trickery and put Him to death. But they said, "Not during the feast, lest there be an uproar of the people (Mk.14:1-2 NKJV)."*

Dinner at Simon's House

The curtains to Jesus' ministry were slowly drawing closed.

The religious leaders were on the warpath. They had tried every trick in the book to trap Jesus and still came up empty. They couldn't just seize him and throw him in jail for fear of what the town people might do. One bad move could compromise everything. A riot could break out. If a riot broke out the Romans would come storming in. Time was closing in. It was two days before the Passover. Something had to break! They needed a window of opportunity soon.

According to Mark, Jesus was in Bethany when the Pharisees and Sadducees got the break they wanted. **Bethany was the home of Mary, Martha and Lazarus, located about a mile from Bethphage and two miles from Jerusalem. Bethany means house of figs.** Jesus had escaped to Bethany to hide out from the angry religious leaders. Jesus had quite a circle of friends. He had a friend that loaned him a colt. He had a friend that knew tax collectors. There were many women that helped finance Jesus' ministry. According to Luke, Mary Magdalene, Joanna the wife of Herod's steward Chuza, and Susanna, and many others provided for Jesus out of their resources," (Lk.8:2-3). Later on, another one of Jesus' friends loaned him a room for he and the disciples to eat Passover. It is good to have friends. Simon was another one of Jesus' friends. Simon lived in the town of Bethany, the same town where some of Jesus other friends lived, Mary, Martha, and their brother Lazarus. Simon used to be a leper. Leprosy was a deadly disease. Lepers were not allowed to be around other people. They were outcast and banished from the community. Lepers lived in Lepersville, a community where other lepers lived. Whenever lepers were in the vicinity of other people they had to shout out, "Unclean." However, Jesus healed Simon of leprosy. Simon may have been the leper that returned and thanked Jesus when he healed ten lepers. The leper thanked Jesus and promised that he would never forget him. He went on his way and did as the Mosaic Law prescribed and showed himself to the priest. Simon was back at home with family and friends. He wanted to thank Jesus for healing him. Simon prepared a dinner and Jesus was the special guest.

A Special Guest at Dinner

The table was set. Guests reclined, glasses clinked, silverware tinkled, plates clattered, and everyone shared in small talk and laughter and settled down to enjoy the moment and music in the background. It was a wonderful evening sitting in the courtyard. A nice soft breeze blew. Everybody that is somebody came to dine with Simon. Simon brought out his best china. The servants poured his best wine, Chardonnay, Merloe, Ernest and Julio, Cabronet Sauvignon, Chateau Brignon. The chef prepared his best dinner.

Jesus was about to cut into his filet mignon and wash it down with a dash of wine, when Miss. Grace walked in. When she stepped into the room everything stopped. The dining stopped. The talking stopped. The laughter stopped. Time stood still as she gracefully made her way to Jesus. Her eyes were like dotted pearls. Her teeth were like ivory. Her hair was black as raven feathers. She walked with style and class and finesse. All eyes were on her. First, women were not invited to banquets. Jewish rabbis did not speak to women in public, nor did they eat with them in public. She was not from the well-to-do crowd. Luke called her a sinner (Lk.7:36-39. She didn't belong and she didn't fit.

Many of us have been in some places where other people thought we did not belong. My wife and I have been in some places where people looked at us as if we did not belong there. Upon receiving the appointment to serve at a certain church whispers and murmurs circulated. Society has a way of branding people, telling us where we fit and where we don't fit, where we belong and where we don't belong, what we can do and what we can't do. We have been in places where people quietly and slyly make their way across the room to ask, "How did you get in here?" They see you dining in a Five Star restaurant and want to know what you are doing there. They see you in an affluent neighborhood and want to know who you know that lives there. They see you at an invitation only affair and want to know who invited you. They see you in an executive suite and want to know how you got the job. They see you in the bank and want to know where you got money. People look at you and want to know how you got blessed. Last time they saw you, you were about to lose your mind, you were having a pity party, about to pull your hair out. The word was out that you weren't going to make it. Some-times we can't seem to get away from the haters. But somehow you got into the room with Jesus.

The woman heard that Jesus was in the room and made a mad dash to get to Jesus. She didn't care who was looking. She didn't care what people thought about her, said about her, and who pointed the finger at her. She wanted to see Jesus. She knew that if Jesus was in the room it was okay for her to come in and that nobody was going to put her out. Since Jesus was in room she was certain to get what she came for. Miss. Grace did not come into the room empty handed. She brought her burdens. She brought her brokenness. She brought her sins. She brought her past.

The woman also brought something to bless Jesus. Some people show up at worship and have a good time. They sing, shout, play church music, flip over the pews, and are so oiled up with the anointing that they fall out in the spirit and slide around the corner and never bring anything to bless the Lord. This woman brought the best thing she had. She brought some perfume that took a year's wages to buy and poured it all over Jesus. The sweet smell filled the room. This woman brought sweetness into the room. She brought joy into the room. She brought happiness into the room. She blessed the room and left the room blessed. We should watch what we bring into the rooms we enter. Bring sweetness and blessings into the rooms you enter.

Slipping into Darkness

However, what the woman did, pouring all that expensive perfume on Jesus, did not sit well with the religious leaders. Neither did it sit well with one of Jesus' disciples (Mk. 14:10). One of the disciples got upset and ticked-off. He shouted and complained that the perfume was too expensive to waste on the preacher and that the money should have been given to the poor. Here Mark connects the loss of money in the Temple with the extravagance spent on Jesus by the expensive perfume. It is so unfortunate that other professions can prosper and live large, but the preacher is expected to live in poverty. I have heard church folk talk about their son or daughter who just graduated from college and landed a good job, with good pay, a company car, housing and an expense account and in the same breath claim, "We are paying the preacher too much."

Some of the religious leaders were at Simon's house when this happened. They saw the disciple storm out of the room. He was the treasurer. He kept up with the money and took some for himself every chance he got. He was a thief and had gotten upset because he did not get his hands on the money for the perfume.

Looking over his shoulder to make sure he was not being followed, the disciple went around one corner and then another. He followed a path down a dark alley, knocked on the door of a dimly lighted house. The door cracked opened and Judas slipped in. "I'll do it," said Judas." "You will do what," whispered the voice inside the house." Judas said it again. "I'll do it," he said, trying to lower his voice and control himself. "Jesus!" "I hear that you want to get rid of Jesus." "I will deliver him to you." "Are you sure that you can do it?" "We have only one shot at this and we do not need any mess-up and mistakes." "I said I will do it." Someone went into a room in the house and after a few minutes came and handed Judas a bag of money, thirty pieces of silver as agreed, almost two hundred thousand dollars in today's currency. Judas grabbed the bag, tucked it in his robe and ran off into the night.

Mark calls our attention to the hatred expressed by the religious leaders and Judas and the loved expressed by this sinful woman. Our love for Jesus is best expressed by what we are willing to give him. The woman gave Jesus her best. Jesus gave the woman his best. She received forgiveness of her sins. She got a new lease on life. Her faith got her a place in the greatest love story ever written. Too often many people feel like "this is too much to give to the Lord." We should give him the best of everything.

Rooms for Rent

The Passover had come. Booths lined the streets of Jerusalem. People were everywhere. I recall going into the Old City of David while we were in Israel. Walk ways are narrow and winding. Booths and parlors and markets were everywhere. Frankincense filled the air. Racks of lamb were everywhere. People were buying and selling everywhere. Likewise, Jerusalem was full of people during Passover. Jesus sent two of the disciples to Jerusalem to make arrangements for the Passover.

According to Luke, the two disciples were Peter and John, (Mk.14:12. Lk.22:7) Bethany was about two to three miles from Jerusalem. He told them that they would see a man carrying a water pot. The man would be easy to recognize because it was customary for women to carry water pots. Finding a place to stay and eat in Jerusalem during the Passover is like attending the Masters in Augusta Georgia.[47] It was a Jewish custom that anyone in Jerusalem who had a room available would give it upon request to celebrate the Passover. The Passover consisted of unleavened bread, wine, bitter herbs, sauce and lamb.[48] When the disciples met the man and told him what Jesus needed, he gave them a key to the upper chamber of his home. **In Jewish culture the upper-room was considered to be especially accommodating for guests. It was a chamber built on the roofs of houses and used in the summer because it was cooler than the regular living quarters.**[49]

In the Upper Room

The disciples did as Jesus told them and went and made preparations for the Passover. Once they settled in the upper room, the disciples are shocked at what Jesus had to say. "One of you will betray me!" However, to get a better feel of how this played out, we should call upon John, the fourth gospel writer, to help us out. John the beloved disciple of Jesus was an eyewitness (Jn.13).

The disciples were in the upper room with Jesus. Judas was also present reclining at the table with the rest. The Devil had already gotten Judas to cut a deal to betray Jesus (Jn.13:1-3). Before they ate the Passover Jesus got up from the table, poured water into a basin and began to wash the disciple's feet. It was customary for the host to wash the feet of his guests (Gen.18:4, 19:2, 24:32, Jn.13:1-38 I Tim. 5:10). Jesus washed all the disciple's feet, James, John, Matthew and the rest. Peter refused to allow Jesus to wash his feet. Jesus told him that if he did not wash his feet he had no part with him. Here we see a humorous side of Peter. When Peter heard what Jesus said he acted as if he was going to undress and get in the bathtub. Peter replied, "Lord, not just my feet but my hands and my head (Jn. 13:7-9)." Jesus even washed Judas' feet. What a marvelous demonstration of grace. This was Judas' chance to change his mind, give the money back and bow out. Judas had been in some dark and dirty places. Yet Jesus was willing to wash his feet in spite of where he had been.

Talking in Circles

Suddenly, Jesus began to talk in circles as he finished up washing the disciples feet. He said that somebody in the room was dirty. "And you are clean, though not every one of you (Jn.13:10-11)." This was another chance for Judas to recant. He washed Judas' feet to say it is not too late to turn back. He let Judas know that he knew something was not right. When Jesus finished washing their feet, he put his clothes back on and returned to his place. They began eating the Passover meal. As Jesus and the disciples observed the Passover, Jesus instituted what the apostles later established as the Lord's Supper, and Holy Communion, (Mk.14:22).

However, Jesus did not drop the issue about somebody not being clean. He began to act out of character. Trouble was written all over Jesus' face. It was evident that something bothered him. Then he said it. "One of you is going to betray me." Silence filled the room.

The disciples started looking around at each other. Peter signaled to John who was reclining near Jesus to ask who it was. John leaned back and whispered to Jesus, Lord is it I (Jn.13:25)?

Jesus touched the lives of many people. He brought hope in the midst of hopeless situations. He showed compassion. After all that Jesus had done, one of his own disciples was going to sell him out. The entire room was filled with noise as one voice shouted over the other, "Lord, is it I?" There are many ways that we can betray the Lord. We can betray him for power, popularity, and political gain. We can betray him for position, status, and money. We too should examine ourselves, "Lord, is it I?" Jesus did not leave the disciples in suspense. "Jesus said, "You will see after I dip this bread in the bitter herbs. The one that eats is the one that will betray me." Imagine the tension in the room. The disciples were on eggshells. They were on the edge of their seat. Some of them even lost their appetite. You could hear their hearts beating. This was another chance for Judas to repent.

I Confess

This would have been a good time for a Perry Mason confession. I liked watching Perry Mason just to hear the culprit shout out, "Okay, I did it!"[50] But Judas did not do that. Jesus dipped the bread and gave it to Judas and told him to go and do what he needed to do quickly. Judas went out into the night, (Jn.13:27-30). Things did not have to go the way they did. Jesus wanted Judas to confess and repent. He was not beyond restoration. Maybe Judas was too fearful of what Jesus might do and what the disciples might say if he spoke up. His pride wouldn't let him speak up. He was too bitter with Jesus. However, we position ourselves for restoration when we release fearfulness, pride and bitterness. The Lord gives us chance after chance to think through bad choices.

Lesson Review

1. How do you respond to people who may have a disease?

2. What can we learn from the woman that anointed Jesus?

3. What Christian celebration came from the Passover?

4. What is the name of the disciple that betrayed Jesus?

5. How many times did Jesus try to persuade Judas?

6. Discuss a time you felt betrayed.

The Stairway to Heaven

Then they came to a place which was named Gethsemane; and He said to His disciples, "Sit here while I pray." And He took Peter, James, and John with Him, and He began to be troubled and deeply distressed. Then He said to them, "My soul is exceedingly sorrowful, even to death. Stay here and watch." He went a little farther, and fell on the ground, and prayed that if it were possible, the hour might pass from Him. And He said, "Abba, Father, all things are possible for you. Take this cup away from me; nevertheless, not what I will, but what you will." (Mk. 14:32-36, NKJV).

Jesus and the Disciples in the Garden of Gethsemane

After the Passover meal, Jesus and the disciples went out the upper room singing. Night had fallen. Dark clouds drifted across the sky. There was not a star out anywhere. The moon barely peeked through the dark clouds. There was an unusual silence as they crossed the Kiddron Valley and entered into an olive orchard near the Mt of Olives. The Garden of Gethsemane was there. **Gethsemane was an olive orchard. The name means "oil press" or "crushing place." It is a place or occasion of great mental or spiritual suffering. Gethsemane is the place where Jesus was arrested.** [51] Gethsemane was Jesus' favorite place to pray. Jesus was a man of prayer. He arose early in the mornings and resorted to a solitary place to pray (Mk.1:35-37). He prayed all night before choosing his disciples, (Lk. 6:12) He taught the disciples to pray. He told them that they should always pray and not faint. He told them that some things can only be achieved by prayer (Mk. 9:29). Prayer is the stairway to heaven.

However, this time was different for Jesus. He took Peter, James and John with him and told the others to keep watch. Jesus began to pour his heart out to the disciples. Fear and dread overtook him. He was troubled. His mind was troubled. His heart was troubled. His spirit was trouble. He had no idea how this was going to play out. He was at a place that he had never been before. Jesus felt the pressing need to pray. Prayer is always in order. Prayer is the stairway to Heaven. Prayer allows us to talk to God about our situation. We should pray when we are confronted by uncertainties. We should pray when we find ourselves at the crossroads of life.

Sleeping Heavenly Peace

Jesus longed for companionship from his friends and his Father. There is nothing like having friends in the time of distress. Friends can help get you through hard and difficult times. Friends can pray with us. Unfortunately, the disciples did not do well comforting Jesus. When Jesus came back from praying he found them sleeping, Peter included. Peter promised to protect Jesus. He promised to be there for Jesus even if the other disciples abandon him. Many of us have friends like Peter and the crew, who could not be found when we needed them. All of us have friends that started out with good intentions but had very little "stick-to-itness." All of us have friends that talk too much and make promises they cannot keep. My youngest daughter, called home on one occasion upset that her friends had promised to help her move. When moving day came, everybody backed out. Sleep! That is what friends do sometimes. That is what Jesus friends did. They slept. Three times Jesus went and prayed. Every time he returned the disciples were fast asleep.

A Prayer of Agony and Assurance

This was a great disappointment to Jesus. Several times Jesus warned Peter of falling into temptation. Yet Peter and none of the other disciples gave serious thought to what Jesus said. They were tired. They had just finished eating. They had been up all night. They didn't have the slightest idea about what was getting ready to happen. Jesus prayed that His Father would remove the cup. Jesus agonized in the Garden of Gethsemane. The "old school" preacher said, Jesus sweated drops of blood. This was a difficult moment for Jesus. Jesus pleaded that God would abort the mission. But the will of God was preordained from the foundation of the world. God's plan of redemption could not be turned back. It was recorded in eternity. This must have been something awesome to think about. You are about to give your life for the bad and wrong doings of everybody. All you have done is good. And now you have to die for what somebody else did. On top of that, one of your own people is responsible for getting you in this mess. How do you die for somebody that sold you down the river?

Nevertheless, Jesus did not back out. The first part of Jesus prayer is a prayer of agony. "Father, remove this cup." The end of his prayer is a prayer of assurance. "Nevertheless, if it be your will . . ." The latter part of the prayer says it is going to be alright. It says I have confidence that God knows best. It says God will give me the courage that I need. When my oldest daughter was greatly ill, I wrestled with God in prayer. I gave God every reason why she needed to stay around. I went some rounds with God. However, I still found myself at the crossroad of "nevertheless." Sometimes God seems to say, you can pray as hard as you like, plead all you will, but I have the last word." That's when we must concede to "nevertheless." "Nevertheless" will help you get through tough times. "Nevertheless" is the life jacket for the storms of life. "Nevertheless" is comfort in a season of discomfort.

The Kiss of Death

Jesus was empowered by his prayer in the Garden of Gethsemane. We are empowered when we pray. Prayer may not always change our situation, but prayer can empower us to endure. Prayer is the stairway to heaven and the heart of God. Jesus woke the disciples and said, "Let's go face destiny" (Mk.14:41-42). Out of the night, amidst the olive trees came a mob armed with swords, clubs, chains, sticks, and daggers. and thronged Jesus. Judas was in the midst of them. The chief priest and elders stood back and watched the plot unfold, (Lk.22:52).

Judas walked up to Jesus grabbed him and kissed him. As soon as that happened the mob seized Jesus. That was the sign that Judas gave the mob. "The one I kiss is Jesus." "Seize him!" It was customary to greet a Rabbi with a kiss. It was a sign of respect and affection for the beloved teacher. However, this was not a kiss of respect, but a kiss of betrayal as well as a kiss of death. Judas' kiss sealed Jesus' fate. There was no turning back once Judas handed Jesus over to the Jewish authorities. They had remained cool. The plot played out to their favor. Jesus was delivered into their hands. They were not about to let him escape.

Show Down in Gethsemane

Caiaphas, the high priest, sent the Temple Guard accompanied by Roman soldiers to arrest Jesus.[52]

However, the disciples refused to go down without a fight. Jesus sensing that something was going to happen had instructed the disciples to get a sword. If you do not have a sword, sell something and get one, he told them (Lk. 22: 35-38). Sure enough, things got out of hand. The disciples drew their swords and a light battle ensued. Swords clashed! The disciples stood their ground and fought for Jesus. In the heat of the battle, one of Jesus' disciples slashed off the ear of the servant of the high priest, (Jn. 18:10).

After letting the guys work off some of their stress and frustration Jesus made the disciples put their swords away, (Lk. 22:51, Jn.18:11). However, Jesus must have been proud of the disciples. They started out as a motley crew, not liking each other, often faithless and fearful. But they rose to the occasion. They were willing to fight for Jesus. What an awesome example of spiritual warfare, the kingdom of darkness against the kingdom of light, the kingdom of God against the kingdom of Satan. As believers we are called to rise to the occasion when our faith is under attack

After the fighting ended, the mob grabbed Jesus and dragged him off into the night. The disciples scattered and hid, fearing for their own lives. As the mob surrounded Jesus and took him into custody, Mark calls our attention to the strange behavior of a certain young man dressed in a linen cloth, who fled the scene naked. Although Matthew and Luke used Mark's account to write their own stories, they did not include this. Obviously, Mark thought it was significant. Some scholars believe that it was the rich young ruler whom Jesus had met earlier (Mk. 10:21, 14:51). Others argue that it was Mark.[53]

Lesson Review

1. What event did the disciples celebrate in the upper room?

2. Discuss how the Lord's Supper is similar to the Passover.

3. Where did Jesus and the disciples go from the upper room?

4. What did the disciples do while Jesus prayed?

5. Who turned Jesus over to the Roman soldiers?

6. Have you ever been sold out by a friend?

7. How did you feel?

Jesus before Pilate

Immediately, in the morning, the chief priests held a consultation with the elders and scribes and the whole council; and they bound Jesus, led Him away, and delivered Him to Pilate. Then Pilate asked Him, "Are You the King of the Jews?" He answered and said to him, "It is as you say." And the chief priests accused Him of many things, but He answered nothing. Then Pilate asked Him again, saying, "Do you answer nothing? See how many things they testify against you!" But Jesus still answered nothing, so that Pilate marveled. Now at the feast he was accustomed to releasing one prisoner to them, whomever they requested. And there was one named Barabbas, who was chained with his fellow rebels; they had committed murder in the rebellion. Then the multitude, crying aloud, began to ask him to do just as he had always done for them. But Pilate answered them, saying, "Do you want me to release to you the King of the Jews?" He knew that the chief priests had handed Him over because of envy. But the chief priests stirred up the crowd, so that he should rather release Barabbas to them. (Mk. 15:1-11).

Order in the Court

After the mob seized Jesus they brought him to Annas and then carried him to the high priest to stand before the Sanhedrin Council (Jn. 18: 12-13). Joseph Caiaphas, the son in law of Annas was the high priest. Caiaphas served as high priest from A.D. 18-36. Caiaphas was the master mind behind the plot.[54] When they brought Jesus in Caiaphas called the council to order. **The Sanhedrin Council was the supreme court of Israel. The council was composed of seventy members, all males, both Sadducees and Pharisees.**[55] The official meeting place of the Sanhedrin was the Hall of the Hewn Stone, located within the Temple precincts. The Sanhedrin Council was governed by a certain set of rules. Any decisions made by the Sanhedrin were not valid anywhere else, except the Hall of the Hewn Stone.[56] First, the court could not meet at night. Secondly, the court could not meet during the time of religious feasts and celebrations. Thirdly, each member of the Sanhedrin was required to give their verdict separately, from the youngest to the oldest. Fourth, the Council could not ask questions that might cause a person to incriminate themselves. Besides, the Sanhedrin did not possess the authority to put anyone to death. Capital punishment was in the hands of Roman government.

The Sanhedrin Council broke all the rules when they held Jesus' trial. They fabricated their testimony. Mark states: "The chief priests and the whole Sanhedrin were looking for evidence against Jesus so they could put him to death. Many testified falsely, but their testimonies did not agree (Mk. 14:55-57). Caiaphas became angry that they could not get anything concrete to hang on Jesus. He got up in Jesus' face and demanded a confession. "Are you the Christ?" Talking about police brutality, the religious leaders worked Jesus over pretty good before they even sent him to Pilate. Then Jesus got beaten by the Romans and later by the bystanders at the cross hurling rocks and insults.

Jesus' response, "I am" satisfied Caiaphas. He needed nothing else. He ripped Jesus clothes and shouted what more do we need! The others spit on Jesus, slapped him around and condemned him to death (Mk. 14: 63-65). Caiaphas prepared the charges to be brought before Pilate. Jesus was charged with sedition and blasphemy. They trumped up charges that Jesus was a political pretender who spoke against Caesar and made claims of being a king. [57] The irony here is that Caiaphas was the high priest. The duty of the high priest was to make a blood sacrifice for the atonement of sin for the people in the Holy of Holies. Here we see Caiaphas, the high priest offering Jesus of Nazareth, the Lamb of God to Pilate to be put to death in the scheme of God's plan to satisfy once and for all the sin of the world.

Warming by the Wrong Fire

As Jesus stood trial, Peter watched at a distance while he warmed by the fire. It was cold out. A crowd had gathered to eavesdrop and see what was going on. To entertain themselves and make things convenient someone built a fire. Someone around the fire recognized Peter and said, "Don't I know you?" "Look like I have seen you before!" "You are one of them that were with Jesus." "You are one of his disciples." "The way you talk gave you away." You don't act like everybody else around the fire. We don't hear you cursing and shouting like everybody else. The mob warming by the fire recognized Peter. The mob recognized several things that caused them to connect Peter to Jesus. They recognized his face. They had seen Peter with Jesus and the other disciples before. They recognized him by his speech. Peter was from Galilee and spoke a different dialect from a Judean. They recognized him by his behavior. But Peter lost it trying to fit in. This was a great chance to say something good about Jesus. This was a great chance for Peter to witness to the crowd around the fire. Instead, Peter got to arguing with the people around the fire and started cursing. He swore up and down that he had never seen Jesus and knew nothing about the man. However, we should not be too hard on Peter. Others have also denied Jesus trying to fit in. Mark reveals what happens when we cease to be near Jesus. We follow at a distance and warm by the wrong fire.

However, Peter was not pleased with his actions. He wept bitterly that he had let Jesus down (Mk. 14:66-72, Mk.15). Peter's response to his actions was totally different than Judas' response. Judas refused to repent. He showed no remorse for his actions. Instead of weeping bitterly and seeking forgiveness he hung himself. Peter wept! He was ashamed and embarrassed. Peter thought that he was strong He thought he had it all together. He thought he had the power to resist. Peter discovered that he was powerless without Jesus. However, Peter realized that even though he messed up it was not the end of the world. We are no different. There are times when we think we are strong enough to do things in our own strength only to discover that we are powerless without Jesus. We should remember that the world does not have to end because we made a bad choice. We too can recover like Peter.

I Find no Fault

After holding their "kangaroo court" the night before, the Sanhedrin Council delivered Jesus to Pontius Pilate early the next morning. Caiaphas was certain that the charges against Jesus would stick and get him an audience with Pilate.[58] Pontius Pilate was a Roman official that served as governor of Israel. The birth date of Pilate is unknown. However, he may have been born near the time of Jesus. He is believed to have come from Central Italy. He served from 26AD-36AD. Pontius Pilate was appointed by the Caesar. **Caesar was the title given to the emperors of Rome. For example, there was Augustus Caesar, Claudius Caesar, etc. Julius Caesar was the most prominent of Rome's emperors.** Tiberius Caesar was emperor of Rome at the time that Pilate was sent to serve as governor of the provinces Judaea, Samaria and Idumæa. (Lk. 3:1). [59]

Pilate was responsible for collecting taxes and overseeing construction projects sanctioned by Rome. However, Pilate's major role was to maintain law and order. Pilate fulfilled his responsibilities by any means necessary. He used brute force whenever his orders were not obeyed and observed peacefully. Pilate possessed the sole authority to order the execution of criminals.[60] Pilate was in Jerusalem during the Passover. Roman military units were on call. A garrison of Roman soldiers was housed near the Court of the Gentiles. **A garrison is an established military post. A Roman garrison was composed of about six hundred soldiers.**[61] The Romans were always on edge due to the increased number of people in Jerusalem. There was always the potential of riots and rebellions at Passover. Six hundred Roman soldiers were always on call in the event something happened.

The Jewish rulers brought Jesus to Pilate and charged him with sedition. They said that Jesus made claims of being king of the Jews. This was a political charge that would get Pilate's attention. After interrogating Jesus, Pilate sent him to Herod Antipas (Luke 23:6-12). Herod sent Jesus back to Pilate.

Pilate was caught between a rock and a hard place. So Pilate decided to give Jesus a few lashings and let him go. The crowd went wild. "If you let this man go, you are no friend to Caesar," (Jn.19:12). "Pilate knew that Jesus had not done anything wrong. However, he wanted to appease the people and the religious leaders of Israel. Pilate had already had a few run-ins with the Jewish religious leaders. First, upon being appointed governor, Pilate came into the city by night bearing the images of Rome, known as standards. The Jews saw this as a slap in the face and total disregard for Jewish Law which opposed the making and bearing of images. Against the Jew's request Pilate refused to move the images.

In protest, the Jews prostrated themselves around Pilate's house for five days and did not move. The following day Pilate commanded a group of Roman soldiers to surround the rebels and prepare to have them executed. The Jews thrust their necks forward and made it known that they were ready to die rather than violate the Law. Stunned by their faith, Pilate had the images removed from

Jerusalem. Another incident emerged when Pilate wanted to honor the emperor in Jerusalem. He brought images of Tiberius and hung them in Herod's palace. The Sanhedrin Council called his hand on it. Shortly after, Emperor Tiberius sent orders to have the shields removed and placed in the Temple of Augustus. Pilate was a lame duck when it came to releasing Jesus. The Jews knew that they could make Pilate back down. All they had to do was threaten to report him to Caesar. Pilate's wife even told him that she had had a dream about Jesus and warned him to have nothing to do with him. Pilate was cornered by destiny. After hearing the deliberations and the charges against Jesus, Pilate said, "I find no fault in him." Pilate was ready to dismiss the charges and release Jesus. But fate weaved her web. God's divine plan of redemption was unfolding.[62]

It was customary for the Romans to release a prisoner during Passover. "Give us Barabbas!" The mob picked up the cadence, "Barabbas, Barabbas, we want Barabbas!" Barabbas was a revolutionist that had been accused of trying to overthrow Rome. Pilate pleased the crowd and let Barabbas go and took Jesus prisoner. Barabbas represents all of us. In spite of how messed up we are, what we have done and how far we have fallen, we have been released. Barabbas is one among many for whom place Jesus took. Roman soldiers seized Jesus. Pushing and shoving Jesus they hustled him into the Praetorian where Pilate was living. **The Praetorian was the official residence of the Roman governor protected by the Praetorian Guard, a distinguished military guard for Roman officials. The Praetorian was the common hall or judgment hall within the governors house, located in Herod's palace (Mk. 15:16, Matt. 27:27, Jn. 18:28, 33, 19:9; Acts 23:35, Phil. 1:13).**[63]

The Roman soldiers amused themselves with Jesus. They took turns making fun of him. Mark gives a graphic account of what happened. They mocked him. They clothed him in purple. They placed a crown of thorns on his head and saluted him. They struck him and spat on him. They led him to be crucified (Mk. 15:20).

Pilate wrote his place in history as the man that had Jesus crucified. Pilate's decision to have Jesus crucified was a grave miscarriage of justice. After Jesus' crucifixion, Pilate was removed from office and returned to Rome. [64]

Lesson Review

1. What was the name of the Jewish council that charged Jesus?

2. Define and discuss miscarried justice.

3. Discuss a situation that you know someone was falsely accused.

4. Discuss several rules that the Sanhedrin broke at Jesus' trial.

5. Who was the Roman governor that sentenced Jesus?

Dead, but Not Done

Now when the sixth hour had come, there was darkness over the whole land until the ninth hour. And at the ninth hour Jesus cried out with a loud voice, saying, "Eloi, Eloi, lama sabachthani?" which is translated, "My God, My God, why have you forsaken me?" Some of those who stood by, when they heard that, said, "Look, He is calling for Elijah!" Then someone ran and filled a sponge full of sour wine, put it on a reed, and offered it to Him to drink, saying, "Let Him alone; let us see if Elijah will come to take Him down." And Jesus cried out with a loud voice, and breathed His last. Then the veil of the temple was torn in two from top to bottom. So when the centurion, who stood opposite Him, saw that He cried out like this and breathed His last, he said, "Truly this Man was the Son of God!" There were also women looking on from afar, among whom were Mary Magdalene, Mary the mother of James the Less and of Joses, and Salome, who also followed Him and ministered to Him when He was in Galilee, and many other women who came up with Him to Jerusalem (Mk.15:33-41, NKJV).

Hey You, Pick Up that Cross

Execution by crucifixion was started by the Assyrians and adopted by the Romans to put trouble makers to death. **Crucifixion is the act of crucifying, an execution on a cross. Crucifixion was an**

extremely painful and torturous form of suffering. [65] It was common to see bodies of crucified criminals hanging from crosses strewn across the hillsides. Golgotha had seen more than its share of crucifixions. Skulls and bones were scattered everywhere. After mocking Jesus the Roman soldiers carried him out to be crucified. It was customary for criminals to carry their cross to the place of execution. The criminal was placed in the center of four Roman soldiers, one up front, one on each side and the other in the rear. The soldier in front carried a board with an inscription that stated the criminal's crime. The inscription was nailed to the cross. Jesus inscription said, "King of the Jews."

Armed with spears, swords, and shields the Romans took the longest route to the crucifixion site. They paraded troublemakers through the streets. They took every street and turned every corner in order that everybody could see what happened to troublemakers. "Do not speak against Caesar!" They sent a message to anybody thinking about leading a riot. The route Jesus took is called the "Via Dolorosa" the "Road of Sorrow."[66] During the visit to Israel we got to see a reenactment of the route Jesus walked through the city to Golgotha. On the way Jesus buckled beneath the weight of the cross. A Roman soldier gave the command, "Pick it up!" Jesus, weak from being beaten and interrogated all night and having not slept, struggling slowly got up with the cross. After going a distance farther Jesus fell to the earth again. The cross fell on Jesus. "Get up, shouted the Roman soldier!" Get up!" Jesus laid there! The Roman soldiers grabbed Jesus, stood him up and several others lifted the cross and thrust it upon Jesus. Take it! One of them shouted. Again, Jesus took the cross and dragged it down the Via Dolorosa. It wasn't long before Jesus went down again.

The crowd was thick. People were stretched out all along the road. No one lifted a hand. No one stepped out into the street to say anything on behalf of the man that had preached good news, healed their sick, and cast out demons that terrorized the community. Nobody did anything. Many of them threw things at the prisoners. Many of them hurled ugly remarks. Many of them spit into the streets. The Roman soldiers were determined to get Jesus to the execution site. They looked into the crowd to see who they might call to help carry Jesus' cross.

They called a man out of the thicket of the crowd, an African by the name of Simon (Lk.23:26). Simon was from Cyrene. **Cyrene was an ancient city located in N. Africa on the Mediterranean in NE Libya.**[67] Simon was in Jerusalem for Passover. He was there to celebrate and share in the festivities. However, Simon's plans were interrupted when Roman soldiers called him out of the crowd, "Hey you, pick up that cross!" At the command of the Roman centurion, Simon stepped out of the crowd, tussling with Jesus' cross, carried to the hill of crucifixion. Simon represents the unexpected crosses that we are compelled to bear. Life does not always go according to our plans. Many of our lives have been interrupted by unexpected crosses. We may have been compelled to bear the cross of an unexpected sickness, and unexpected loss, an unexpected burden. Dolores and I know what it means to bear the cross of unexpected burdens. I am sure many of you know what I'm talking about. For example when your grown children say I'm moving back home for awhile. Or I need you to keep the kids. Or put me on your Verizon, Sprint or AT&T plan. However, all of us, like Simon take up the crosses of life.

Crucified Among Thieves

Roman soldiers marched Jesus to Golgotha, "the Place of a Skull" to be crucified. Golgotha is the Greek name for the place where Jesus was crucified and "Calvary" is the Latin. Golgotha was shaped like a skull. Once they reached the place of execution, the criminal was made to lie down on the cross while Roman soldiers nailed the hands. The feet were loosely bound. A piece of wood called a "saddle" was placed between the criminal's legs to support his weight and keep the nails from tearing through the flesh. This also caused the lungs to collapse causing asphyxiation. The cross was lifted up and dropped in the ground. A wooden placard was placed over the head of the criminal announcing the crime. The criminal was left to die. Sometimes it took prisoners weeks to die. Crucified criminals slowly died from hunger and thirst, and the scorching heat. Some criminals went mad before they died. Birds of prey and wild beast feasted upon dying criminals hanging from crosses.

It was customary to help ease the pain of dying criminals by giving them wine to drink. But Jesus refused to take anything to soothe the pain. Jesus was resolved to taste the bitterness of death (Mk. 15:33-36). While Jesus died on the cross, the soldiers threw dice for his clothes. Jews wore five articles of clothing: an under garment, an outer robe, sandals, girdle and turban. Jesus' entire life was lived keeping company with sinners. Even at the end he was in the company of sinners. Two other men were also crucified with Jesus. They were thieves. Neither Mark nor the other gospel writers give their names. However other sources refer to them as Demas and Gestas. The Romans put many people to death but did not maintain records of them unless they were executed for a crime against Rome. Demas and Gestas went around terrorizing and robbing people. They hid in caves and waited for travelers and strangers to come by and took what they wanted.

One of the thieves made fun of Jesus. You can hear him taunting Jesus. "I know your story is like everybody else, they got the wrong guy. Sure! Me too! "And if you really are some kind of savior then save yourself and us." But the other thief knew that he did not deserve mercy. He knew that he has lived a reckless life and admitted that he deserved to be punished. The thieves no doubt had heard about Jesus. Thief says to Jesus, "When you come into your kingdom, remember me!" That should be our attitude. "I don't claim to be right." "I don't claim to have it all together, but remember me! I know I don't deserve it, but remember me."

The crucifixion of Jesus was a tragic miscarriage of justice. Religious leaders obsessed by their traditions weaved a conspiracy to have Jesus put to death. They were unwilling to change. They resented Jesus for pointing out their hypocrisy. On the other hand, the crucifixion of Jesus reveals the risks one takes when rising against systems of power and oppression. Power brokers do not give up willingly. Jesus' retaliation against injustice is evidence of the cost one might expect to pay. Mark portrays Jesus as a radical, a revolutionist, who went against the grain. Jesus refused to play religion with the religious leaders in light of their traditions and unjust laws. Jesus shows us what we can expect when we seriously follow him. Following Jesus can be dangerous. John Huss, John Wycliff, Joan of Arc, Martin Luther, Dr. Martin Luther King, Malcolm X, Nelson Mandela and others found this out. Although Jesus' death was the result of a political conspiracy orchestrated by evil men it was the fulfillment of God's divine plan to settle the debt of sin and reconciled humankind to God.

Spectators at the Cross

As Jesus hanged from the cross a crowd gathered to watch. The religious leaders watched. Those that had endeared themselves to him watched. Those that did not know him watched. As Jesus died a series of events unfolded. Jesus cried out from the cross. **"Eloi, Eloi, lama sabachthani," which means "My God, My God, why have you forsaken me?** According to Mark, these are the first words uttered by Jesus from the cross. Mark suggests that the phrase is neither Hebrew nor Greek, but Aramaic. Aramaic was the common language used among Jews.[68] As the crowd stood at the foot of the cross mocking Jesus and poking fun, they murmured to each other, "He is calling for Elijah." Let's sit here and see whether Elijah shows up.

However, in the midst of their waiting the sky darkened. It became midnight at day light. The sun refused to shine. Lightning and thundering filled the sky. All of sudden the Temple curtain rent from top to bottom. In previous times, the priest entered the Holy of Holies once a year to offer atonement for the sins of the people. However, the rent curtain was a sign that Jesus was the ultimate sacrifice and that every believer was granted access to God, both Jew and Gentile. The women that followed Jesus were also at the foot of the cross when Jesus cried out and when the Temple curtain rent. They had accompanied him on many of his preaching ventures. They remained with him to the end. A Roman centurion and other Roman soldiers were stationed at the foot of the cross. **A Centurion was the commander of a century in the Roman army. A century was composed of a hundred men.**[69]

One of the soldiers offered Jesus hyssop to help comfort and ease the pain. Another soldier took his spear a pierced Jesus in the side and released a fountain of blood that flowed down the rugged hill of Golgotha. Cloaked in darkness, heaven covered the dark, gloomy hill with tears of sorrow as God watched his son die on the cross. In the midst of the darkness, the messianic secret is revealed by the confession of a Roman centurion, "Surely this was the son of God".

Lesson Review

1. Who invented crucifixion?

2. What was the route called that Jesus took to be crucified?

3. Give the Latin and Hebrew name of where Jesus was crucified.

4. What was the name of the man that carried Jesus cross?

5. What city was the man from that carried Jesus cross?

LESSON 13

Early Sunday Morning

Now when the Sabbath was past, Mary Magdalene, Mary the mother of James, and Salome bought spices, that they might come and anoint Him. Very early in the morning, on the first day of the week, they came to the tomb when the sun had risen. And they said among themselves, "Who will roll away the stone from the door of the tomb for us?" But when they looked up, they saw that the stone had been rolled away—for it was very large. And entering the tomb, they saw a young man clothed in a long white robe sitting on the right side; and they were alarmed. But he said to them, "Do not be alarmed. You seek Jesus of Nazareth, who was crucified. He is risen! He is not here. See the place where they laid Him. But go, tell His disciples and Peter that He is going before you into Galilee; there you will see Him, as He said to you (Mk. 16:1-7, NKJV)."

Good Riddance

After Jesus was crucified, dead and buried the crowd scattered. The disciples fled. The women went home grieving. The Romans were content to rid themselves of another troublemaker. The Pharisees and Sadducees dusted their hands, satisfied that they had silenced Jesus. It was over! They could get back to business as usual. Many of the women that supported Jesus ministry watched the Roman's put him to death. They heard the ringing of the hammer driving nails into Jesus hands. They watched as the crowd poked fun at him. They saw the centurion pierce Jesus side. They saw the blood come streaming down. They watched him hang his head and die. They watched as Joseph and Nicodemus came and took Jesus down from the cross and lay the beaten, bruised, battered, bloody Jesus in the tomb (John 19:38-42). However, even though Jesus was dead, that was not the end. God's redemption plan was not complete.

The women refused to be out done. They went home and waited the Sabbath out. They went and caught some sleep. Sometimes you have got to just sleep it off! Sleep off your frustration. Sleep off your anxiety. Sleep off your shattered hopes. The next morning, after the Sabbath was over, they got up and headed to the tomb to anoint Jesus' body for burial. They slipped into the night. They risked being spotted. However, as they made their way, they became troubled when they remembered that a huge stone had been rolled into the mouth of the tomb. The Romans had also placed a seal on the tomb. There was no way that they were going to be able to roll the stone away.

Rolling Stones

However, when they got to the place where Jesus was buried, the stone was rolled away and the tomb was empty. This is an encouragement to those who find themselves overwhelmed by circumstances out of their control. The women could have turned around. They could have panicked knowing that the Jewish religious leaders as well as the Roman authorities were on patrol. But instead, they kept walking. When they arrived the stone had already been rolled away. The Lord is still rolling stones away. Go forward in faith and when you get where you are going the Lord has already worked it out. When the women arrived two men were sitting where Jesus had been buried. They told the women that Jesus had risen and would meet the disciples and Peter in Galilee (Mk. 16:1-7).

Mark ended Jesus earthly ministry with the glorious announcement, "He is arisen!" The crucified Christ is the risen Christ. After the resurrection, Jesus made many appearances to the disciples. He appeared to Mary Magdalene. He appeared to two heartbroken disciples on the Emmaus road. They were fearful that they would be next. It was dangerous to stay in Jerusalem. One evening Jesus appeared to the disciples. Jesus continues to show up when we are at our lowest point and feel like the world has ended and we have nothing else to live for. Sunday morning changed Friday's tragedy. God got the last word. Every "Good Friday" has an Easter Sunday. Every crucifixion has a resurrection. The religious leaders did not realize that Jesus' death on the cross was God's divine plan to redeem humanity. The cross that appeared to be a scandal and a disgrace became the emblem of victory and triumph. The cross broke down the wall that separated Jews and Gentiles. The cross reconciled humankind to God. The cross broke the power of sin and the power of Satan. The resurrection broke the power of Death and the grave. To the wise, the preaching of the cross is foolishness, but to them that believe it is the power of God unto salvation. What looked like a tragedy was a triumph. Jesus resurrection says that we can rise from seemingly dead end situations. Paul said, "Without the resurrection our faith is vain", (1Cor. 15:13-20; 29-32).

Appearances of Jesus after the Resurrection

Event	Matt	Mark	Luke	John
Myrrh Bearers	**28:1**	**16:1**	**24:1**	
The Empty Tomb	**28:2-8**	**16:2-8**	**24:2-12**	**20:1-13**
Resurrection	**28:9-10**		**24:1-8**	**20:14-16**
Noli me tangere	**"Touch**	**Me**	**Not!"**	**20:17-17**
Emmaus Road	**16:12-13**		**24:13-32**	
To the Apostles			**24:36-43**	**20:19-20**

Great Commission	28:16-20	16:14-18	24:44-49	20:21-23
Doubting Thomas				20:24-29
The Ascension		16:19-20		24:50-53

Lesson Review

1. What is the glorious news of Mark's gospel?

2. Who was the first person to see Jesus after the resurrection?

3. Why were the women at Jesus tomb?

4. List some appearances after Jesus resurrection?

5. What evidence does the believer have of Jesus resurrection?

The Miracles of Jesus in the Gospels

Miracles	Matt	Mark	Luke	John
Jesus Turns Water to Wine				2:1-11
Jesus Heals an Official's Son				4:43-54
Jesus Drives Out an Evil Spirit		1:21-27	4:31-36	
Jesus Heals Peter's Mother-in-Law	8:14-15	1:29-31	4:38-39	
Jesus Heals Many Sick at Evening	8:16-17	1:32-34	4:40-41	

First Miraculous Catch of Fish			5:1-11	
Jesus Cleanses a Man With Leprosy	8:1-4	1:40-45	5:12-14	
Jesus Heals a Centurion's Servant	8:5-13		7:1-10	
Jesus Heals a Paralytic	9:1-8	2:1-12	5:17-12	
Jesus Heals a Man's Withered Hand	12:9-14	3:1-6	6:6-11	
Jesus Raises a Widow's Son in Nain			7:11-17	
Jesus Calms a Storm	8:23-27	4:35-41	8:22-25	
Jesus Casts Demons into a Herd of Pigs	8:28-33	5:1-20	8:26-39	
Jesus Heals a Woman in the Crowd	9:20-22	5:25-34	8:42-48	
Jesus Raises Jairus' Daughter to Life	9:18, 23-26	5:21-24, 35-43	8:40-42, 49-56	
Jesus Heals Two Blind Men	9:27-31			
Jesus Heals a Man Unable to Speak	9:32-34			
Jesus Heals an Invalid at Bethesda				5:1-15
Jesus Feeds 5,000	14:13-21	6:30-44	9:10-17	6:1-15
Jesus Walks on Water	14:22-33	6:45-52		6:16-21
Jesus Heals Many Sick in Gennesaret	14:34-36	6:53-56		
Jesus Heals a Gentile Woman's daughter	5:21-28	7:24-30		

		7:31-37		
Jesus Heals a Deaf and Dumb Man		7:31-37		
Jesus Feeds 4,000	15:32-39	8:1-13		

Miracles	Matt	Mark	Luke	John
Jesus Heals a Blind Man at Bethsaida		8:22-26		
Jesus Heals a Man Born Blind				9:1-12
Jesus Heals a Boy with a Demon	17:14-20	9:14-29	9:37-43	
Miraculous Temple Tax in a Fish's Mouth	17:24-27			
Jesus Heals a Blind, Mute Demoniac	12:22-23		11:14-23	
Jesus Heals a Crippled Woman			13:10-17	
Jesus Heals a Man With Dropsy on the Sabbath			14:1-6	
Jesus Cleanses Ten Lepers			17:11-19	
Jesus Raises Lazarus from the Dead				11:1-45
Jesus Restores Sight to Bartimaeus	20:29-34	10:46-52	18:35-43	
Jesus Cursed the Fig Tree	21:18:22	11:12-14		
Jesus Heals a Servant's Severed Ear			22:50-51	
Second Miraculous Catch of Fish				21:4-11

Conclusion

The Gospel of Mark gives an action packed account of Jesus' three year ministry. Over half of the Gospel of Mark covers the last two weeks of Jesus' life, known as Passion Week. The Final Straw set out to show how the ongoing controversies between Jesus and the religious leaders and the events of Passion Week sealed Jesus' fate.

Jesus and the disciples went from town to town preaching the good news of the kingdom of God. Jesus appeared on the scene at a time when the people of Israel were looking for something different. The religious leaders had failed the people. Instead of showing compassion toward their needs and conditions, the religious leaders placed unnecessary demands upon the people. They used their authority to weight the people down with religious traditions. Many of the traditions that demanded to be observed were man-made and were not required in the written Law of Moses. Jesus became the voice for the oppressed and took on the religious leaders of Israel by blatantly defying such religious traditions as fasting and ceremonial hand washing. Mark's gospel is therefore not only a gospel of action, but revolutionary action. Mark reveals the radical actions of Jesus which of course did not set well with the Pharisees and Sadducees. The Temple, the Law and the synagogue were sacred cows to them. They felt responsible to protect and maintain the established order.

In their attempt to maintain the established order and Jesus' attempt to enlighten the religious leaders regarding their hypocrisy and misrepresentation of the Law, the two worlds clashed. Jesus and the disciples found themselves in a battle that was impossible to win. They were outnumbered by the religious leaders and their authority. The system was bigger than they were. By becoming the voice of the oppressed Jesus invited himself into a political battle that culminated in the religious leaders conspiring to put him to death. When Jesus did not conform to many of the traditions set forth by the Pharisees and Sadducees, they became relentless in their plan to get rid of him. I tried to avoid the issues of political power and oppression. However, politics and power is what got Jesus crucified.

Mark suggests that systematic power, whether it is religious, social, political, or economic can be uncompromising, lacking in compassion, and difficult to change. Mark suggests that we be prepared to endure what Jesus did if we intend to be his disciples and live out the radical edge that he demonstrated time and time again. Unfortunately, many of us have missed the radical nature of Jesus' ministry. We need our job. We need our ministry. We have bills to pay and family to care for. Therefore, we are content to play it safe, keep quiet and do nothing even when we see oppression and unfairness. However, Jesus was not a candidate for the "Just Go Along Award." So he ended up on a cross. However, the story of Jesus of Nazareth does not end at the cross.

Mark declared that Jesus arose from the dead. Jesus' resurrection says that we can rise above our enemies. It says that we can be victorious even in death if we die for what we believe is just. The resurrection says, we do not have to lie down and die simply because people want us dead. Furthermore, the resurrection says that we can live again even when life looks dark, dismal and disappointing. The same way that God resurrected Jesus from the dead, God is also able to resurrect dead dreams, dead ambitions, dead inspiration and dead hope. AMEN!

Bibliography

Barclay, William. The Gospel of Mark. Philadelphia: Westminster, 2010.

Blaiklock, E. M. The Compact Hand Book of the New Testament. Minneapolis: Bethany House, 2003.

Butler, Trent C. Holman Old Testament Commentary of Isaiah. Tennessee: Broadman and Holman, 2002.

Cooper, Rodney, L. Holman New Testament Commentary of Mark. Nashville: Holman, 2000.

Edersheim, Alfred. Sketches of Jewish Social Life. Massachusetts: Hendrickson, 2009.

Flanders, Jackson Henry Jr. Introduction to The Bible. New York: John Wiley and Sons, 2009.

Tenny, Merrill, C., ed. Pictorial Bible Dictionary. Nashville: Southwestern, 2009.

McGowan, James. The Gospel of Mark: Christ the Servant. Chattanooga: AMG, 2006.

Morrison, Frank. Who Moved the Stone? Grand Rapids: Zondervan, 1996.

Stedman, Ray, C. The Servant Who Rules. Michigan: Discovery House, 2002.

Werner, Kelly. The Bible as History. New York: William Morrow, Barnes & Nobel, 2010.

Wrede, William. The Messianic Secret. Cambridge: James and Clark, 1971.

Wright, Ernest. ed. Great People of the Bible and How They Lived. New York: 2001.

Notes

1   Ernest Wright, ed., Great People of the Bible and How They Lived, (New York:2001), 300.

2   Ray C. Stedman The Servant Who Rules, (Michigan: Discovery House, 2002), 7-9.

3   Merrill C. Tenney, ed., Pictorial Bible Dictionary, (Tennessee: Southwestern, 2009), 318.

4   James McGowan, The Gospel of Mark: Christ the Servant (Tennessee: AMG, 2006), 1-6.

5   The New King James Version, the Gospel of Mark 10:45.

6   Henry Jackson Flanders, Jr., Introduction to the Bible, (Baylor: John Wiley and Sons, 2009), 323.

7   William Wrede, The Messianic Secret, (Cambridge: James and Clark, 1971), 9-11.

8   Ernest Wright, ed., 309.

9   Ibid, 331.

10 Ibid, 328.

11 Pictorial Bible Dictionary, 834.

12 Ernest Wright, ed. 358

13 Ibid, 363.

14 E.M. Blaiklock, Compact Handbook of New Testament Life, (Minneapolis: Bethany House, 2003), 105-9.

15 Ibid, 96-100.

16 Ernest Wright, 363.

17 E.M. Blaiklock, 111-16.

18 Ernest Wright, ed., 360

19 Ibid, 360.

20 E. M. Blaiklock, 63.

21 Trent C. Butler, Holman Old Testament Commentary: Isaiah (Tennessee: Broadman and Holman, 2002), 1-3.

22 William Barclay, The Gospel of Luke, (Philadelphia: Westminster, 2010), 10.

23 Pictorial Bible Dictionary, 711.

24 McGowan, 16.

25 Blaiklock, 112-14.

26 Ibid, 817-18.

27 Merriam Webster http://www.merriam- webster.com/dictionary/compassion

28 Shofar is a trumpet made with ram's used in Hebrew religious services.

29 Ray C. Stedman, The Servant Who Rules, (Michigan: Discovery House, 2002), 69-70.

30 Ibid, 73.

31 Ibid, 169.

32 Pictorial Bible Dictionary, 821.

33 Alfred Edersheim, Sketches of Jewish Social Life, (Massachusetts: Hendrickson, 2009), 143-45, 174.

34 Pictorial Bible Dictionary, 182.

35 Stedman, 177.

36 Flanders, 333.

37 Pictorial Bible Dictionary, 735.

38 Blaiklock, 106-7

39 Merriam Webster-On-Line Dictionary

40 McGowan, 111.

41 Blaiklock, 78.

42 Pictorial Bible Dictionary, 298.

43 Ibid, 63.

44 The Biggest Loser is a television Reality Show in which overweight people compete to lose the most weight.

45 Palm Sunday precedes Easter Sunday and is celebrated by the Christian community as the day Jesus road into Jerusalem on a donkey and was declared by the common people of Israel.

46 Pictorial Bible Dictionary-the denarius was a silver Roman coin equal to a penny, 554.43.

47   The Masters is a major golf tournament held in Augusta Georgia and homeowner lease their residence to guests.

48   Pictorial Bible Dictionary, 280.

49   Ibid, 876.

50   Perry Mason is a "who done it" television show that aired in the 70s.

51   Pictorial Bible Dictionary, 310.

52   McGowan, 203.

53   William Barclay, The Gospel of Mark (Philadelphia: Westminster, 2002), 347.

54   McGowan, 206.

55   Pictorial Bible Dictionary, 751-52.

56   Frank Morrison, Who Moved the Stone? (Michigan: Zondervan, 1996), 13-29.

57   McGowan, 208-9.

58   Morrison, 41.

59   Pictorial Bible Dictionary, 135.

60   McGowan, 214.

61   Pictorial Bible Dictionary, 300.

62   Blaiklock, 66.

63   Ibid, 678.

64   Blaiklock, 66-68.

65   Keller Werner, The Bible as History, (New York: William Morrow, Barnes & Nobel, 2010), 229-30.

66   William Barclay, The Gospel of Mark (Philadelphia: Westminster, 2010), 360

67   Pictorial Bible Dictionary, 192.

68   McGowan, 221.

69   Pictorial Bible Dictionary, 150.